How Startups Work With Partners To Sell
More, Add Features, And Get Acquired

THE BOOK ON PARTNER- —SHIPS

FRANZ-JOSEF SCHREPF

Copyright and Disclaimers

The Book On Partnerships: How Startups Work With Partners To Sell More, Add Features, And Get Acquired.

ISBN: 979-8-9912888-1-1

Copyright © 2024 by Franz-Josef Schrepf. All rights reserved.

No part of this book may be reproduced, stored in a retrieval system, or transmitted in any form or by any means, electronic, mechanical, photocopying, recording, or otherwise, without the prior written permission of the author, except in the case of brief quotations.

The information provided in this book is for general informational purposes only and should not be construed as professional advice. The author assumes no responsibility for errors or omissions, or for any loss or damage resulting from the use of the information contained herein.

This book does not provide legal advice. The information contained herein is not a substitute for professional legal advice. Readers should consult a licensed attorney for advice regarding their specific legal issues.

The views expressed in this book are solely those of the author and do not necessarily reflect the views of any other individual or organization. While the author has made every effort to ensure the accuracy and completeness of the information contained in this book, the author assumes no responsibility for errors, inaccuracies, omissions, or any inconsistencies herein.

This book contains references and links to external websites that are not under the control of the author. The author is not responsible for the content or privacy practices of any external websites.

Written with <3 by a human

To Charlotte and Tara.
The most important partners in my life.

WHAT EXPERTS SAY ABOUT THE BOOK ON PARTNERSHIPS

"I wish I had this book back when I built my first partner program. It would have helped me avoid so many painful mistakes that now seem obvious."
— *Nelson Wang, Head of Worldwide Partnerships @ Airtable + Founder of Partner Principles*

"A high-density, fast-paced read by one of our industry's most enthusiastic champions."
— *Jay LeBoeuf, Head of Business Development & Partnerships @ Adobe*

"Where was this book when I started working with partners? It's your roadmap to unlocking new opportunities and accelerating growth with partnerships."
— *Shay Howe, Chief Marketing Officer @ ActiveCampaign*

"The wisdom of the entire partnership community in your pocket."
— *Asher Mathews, CEO @ Partnership Leaders*

"How would you feel if a competitor partnered with the biggest player in your industry? Read this book and beat them to the punch."
— *Jared Fuller, Author of 'NEARBOUND and the Rise of the Who Economy'*

"At G2, our entire business is built around trust. This book will teach you how to build trusted relationships at scale."
— *Christine Li, VP of Global Partnerships @ G2*

"Partners are essentially customers in disguise. This book isn't just about partnerships; it's about boosting your business by embracing those partners who truly understand and appreciate your customers."
— *Daniel O'Leary,*
Senior Director of Partnerships @ Box

"ROI, unit economics, and profitable growth. If any of these matter for your business, you need to invest in partnerships. This book is your guide."
— *Greg Portnoy, CEO @ Euler*

"Product Led Growth and Sales Led Growth motions are amazing, yet true growth and acceleration by 3X and 4X comes from partner-led motions. Just look at Salesforce, AWS, Google, and Microsoft. Partnerships require deep work and collaboration beyond the initial executive alignment. Franz's book is a great place to learn how."
— *Olga Lykova, Head of Partnerships,*
North America @ monday.com

TABLE OF CONTENT

Preface	10
Introduction	16
Chapter 1: Partnership 101	26
What Is A Partnership, Anyway?	27
Why Do Most Partnerships Fail?	38
Your Build, Buy, Partner Strategy	44
How To Find Partnership Opportunities?	51
Ideal Partner Profiles: The 4 Cs of Partnerships	55
When Should You Invest In Partnerships?	64
What Does A Partner Manager Do All Day?	70
Partner Portfolio Management	76
Chapter 2: Marketing Partnerships	82
Don't Boil The Ocean. Shoot Fish In A Barrel.	83

The Four Flavours of Marketing Partnerships　85
Make Your Partner Marketing Pop　89
Level Up Your Marketing Partner Program　96

Chapter 3: Service & Channel Partners　102
Why Do Startups Need Service & Channel Partners?　103
Are You The Right Fit For Your Partners?　109
How To Find Your Partners In Business　113
Overcome Channel Conflict And Win Together　116
From 10 To 1,000 Service & Channel Partners　126

Chapter 4: Product Partnerships　132
Integrations ≠ Partnerships　133
Are You Ready To Build?　137
The Integration Negotiation Tango　142
Co-Selling Strategies With Product Partners　155
Turn Your Partner Program Into An Ecosystem　165

Chapter 5: Alliances　174
How To Move A Market　175
Which Elephant Should You Ask For A Dance?　185
Where To Find The Pieces Of The Alliance Puzzle　190
Negotiation, Execution, And The Heavy Lifting　197
How To Get Your Startup Acquired　204

Chapter 6: Crunch Time	212
Acknowledgements	217
Glossary	221
Endnotes	229
About the Author	243

PREFACE

"The way they are acting shows you the caliber of people they are."
—Our lawyer

Sweat ran down the agency owner's face. He stammered: "I think . . . I'm, I'm sure . . . this is a misunderstanding." His business partner was stressed, too. I caught a glimpse of him as he fidgeted with the collar of his shirt. His breath was heavy. He then turned off his camera to escape the discomfort of the video call.

I paused for dramatic effect, put on a stern face, and said: "I guess we're done here. You'll hear from our lawyers." I pushed a button. The meeting ended. What a relief. For the next few minutes, I stared at a blank screen. Anxiety got the better of me. Again. I was three months into my first partnership role. So far it had been a disaster.

In March 2020 I had shut down my own startup and now had a massive chip on my shoulder. Every failed entrepreneur knows this feeling. That's when our investor, Seedcamp, asked me to help out one of their portfolio companies, Hopin. I was still burnt-out but felt obligated to join this small virtual events startup with less than 20 people. After all, I lost the investor's money. I figured it would be good karma to lend a hand for a bit. That same day, governments around the globe announced their Covid-19 lockdowns. Every single event in the world had to move online. And we were the platform of choice.

Overnight we had product-market-fit. Thousands of customers banged down our door. Every. Single. Day. If you didn't code, you had to sell. Each one of us took more than 20 sales calls per day. We closed deals worth hundreds of thousands of dollars every week. We doubled our team size every month. We drank from the fire hose. Yet, our efforts felt like a drop of water on a hot stone. Little did we know that less than two years later, Hopin would raise $1 billion in funding at a $7.75 billion valuation. According to Sifted, we became the fastest growing startup in European history.[1]

One tired evening after 14 hours of sales calls, my colleague Agustin pointed out a curious fact: 25% of our inbound leads were event agencies. The pandemic had wiped out their entire business. They furloughed their employees and now struggled to survive. That's when it clicked for me: partnerships.

See, we didn't launch our partner program as part of a large, deliberate strategy. It came from a place of desperation. Our bottleneck wasn't our platform. It could host a lot more events. What slowed us down was our lack of manpower. Virtual events were brand new. Customers had tons of questions before they decided to buy our platform. And once they had access, they had even more questions. There was no way we could hire enough people to capture all this demand. I also had no intention of continuing my insane work schedule. So, on my next call with an agency, I said: "I need to sleep. Do you want to take my sales calls for me?"

The agency owner jumped out of his seat. This was a golden opportunity for him to save and even expand their business. The next day our CEO Johnny gave me the green light to test out a partner program. I had no idea how to do this and no time to research. I still had to take my 20 sales calls per day. So, I picked 10 agencies in different countries and experimented. Three months later, it almost ended in a lawsuit.

If you're curious about what happened, you can jump ahead to Chapter 3: Service & Channel Partners. It's a wild story. Full of channel conflict, betrayal, and what we in partnerships refer to as *assholes*. People who push for win-lose outcomes. You can find a detailed definition of this and many other partnership terms in this book's glossary.

In the end, I'm grateful about the incident though. It forced me to get serious and study partnerships. I got obsessed with the question of how to avoid this type of channel conflict. Partnerships look so easy from the outside. How hard can it be to get two companies to work together?

Yet partnerships are a double-edged sword. They give you a lot of leverage. That's because partners act as an extension of your business. Another pair of hands when all hands are on deck. But with great leverage comes great responsibility. If you don't know how to use them, the hands will be clumsy and wreak havoc. As legendary investor Charlie Munger said: "There are three ways a smart person can go broke: liquor, ladies, and leverage."

For the next four years, I talked to hundreds of partnership professionals. Read dozens of books. Attended and spoke at conferences. Started my own podcast called *The Partner Ship*. And I even became the San Francisco chapter host of *Partnership Leaders*, the #1 community in our industry.

This book is my effort to condense all this research into one simple guide for anyone who is new to partnerships. It's the resource I wish I had when I was new to the job.

What's most important though is that I not only talk and write about partnerships, I have also used these ideas in real life scenarios. I am a practitioner who is in the trenches every day. Not a consultant who talks about big ideas and then blames any failure on the implementation. Like a communist. But I digress.

Franz-Josef Schrepf
27th July 2024

INTRODUCTION

"You will get all you want in life, if you help enough other people get what they want."
—Zig Ziglar

Partnerships can make or break your business. For example, after the initial hiccup I mentioned in the preface, Hopin's agency program became a smashing success. I had finally learned how to build a program that worked both for us and our partners. Soon after, our VP of Sales pinged me: "Franz, I saw you're not on the round-robin for new inbound leads. How did you still close $1 million+ this quarter?"

I left her a quick message between calls: "I got my own deal flow." And deal flow I had! Our agency partners sent us dozens of deals and hosted hundreds of events every month. Then we developed a certification program. It allowed us to scale to hundreds of agencies, which generated tens of millions in revenue. These partners were so good, we later even outsourced all our production services to them.

At the same time, Hopin continued its meteoric rise. We signed up thousands of customers including the United Nations, Google, Salesforce, and TechCrunch. All of them hosted global virtual events with millions of attendees. Each successful event fueled our viral growth and the demand for more agencies to provide services around these events.

During this time our customers sent us hundreds of requests for product integrations. That's when I handed over the agency program to focus on our technology partnerships. The next year we launched over 50 integrations and acquired seven startups. Our most notable acquisition was StreamYard, the leading software for non-gaming live streams. Less than two years after our incorporation, Hopin acquired StreamYard for $250 million.[2] It was one of many acquisitions that started out as a product partnership.

The good times didn't last though. I know this is a strange thing to say about a global pandemic. But as COVID restrictions faded away, so did the market for virtual events. Turns out you don't find product-market-fit. You maintain it. The whole company shifted its focus toward StreamYard. Live streaming continued to boom, and we relied on partners to grow our business. Creators used our tool to create their live shows, but they stream them on social media platforms. That's where their audience is, so we had a lot to gain from strategic alliances with the likes of Facebook and YouTube. Those platforms thought so too. LinkedIn even invested up to $50 million into Hopin and StreamYard as part of our engagement.[3]

This information is all public. What isn't public are all the mistakes we made, lessons we learned, and frameworks we developed along the way. Until now. You see, when I started in partnerships, I had to piece together thousands of tiny bits of information. It was a mess. There wasn't a single book I could read or a course I could take to study partnerships. A lot of the resources focused on old school software companies. I read about how to get CD-ROMs shelved at Radio Shack or how to sell software for mainframe computers. Yet not a single book could answer basic questions like "What types of partnerships exist?" or "How do you avoid channel conflict?"

Even seasoned partnership professionals struggle with these questions!

This is a huge, missed opportunity for our industry because partnerships can make or break your business. Entrepreneurs intuitively know this. I see it at every startup event I go to in London or San Francisco. Founders always have a slide in their pitch deck that lists partnerships as a growth lever. This is not an accident.

The goal of any partnership is to create a competitive advantage for both you and your partner.[4] And if there's one thing startups need it is an edge over their competition. There are several ways partners can help you to create a moat around your business. For example, some partners, like VC funds, can give you exclusive access to their audience. In this case, their portfolio companies. It's hard to compete with you if you are the recommended partner of your customer's investor. There's even an added benefit in this case. Because these startups got funded by a VC, you know that they actually have money. Nice.

Other partners like agencies allow you to outsource labor-intensive tasks like sales and support. If done well, these partners allow you to waste less time on hiring. Fewer people means lower overhead costs. And some of them can even help you access new markets where you don't speak the local language. Also nice.

On the flip side, technology companies can be great partners as well. That's because they allow you to add features faster through integrations. This is crucial because the best startups are point solutions. They do one thing really well. They either run like a horse, fly like a sparrow, or swim like a fish. Poor performing startups are ducks. They try to do everything and do nothing well. Partners help you avoid the trap of the "everything platform." They allow you to outsource distractions so you can focus on your core business.

The reasons above explain why the world's largest companies are built around partner ecosystems. Microsoft generates a whopping 95% of its commercial revenue through partners.[5] The iPhone in your pocket is only useful because of the two million apps that partners have built for the Apple App store. Global reach is impossible without partners.

Partnerships can also be a solid exit path for startups. At Hopin, we acquired seven companies. Many of them were partners first. It's easy to see why. With a partner, you have a proven track record working together. You know their team. You know their processes, and you know what your customers think of them. This makes partners a lot less risky to buy than an unknown entity. After all, the vast majority of acquisitions fail. That's why buyers try to de-risk these transactions as much as they can. And if you don't want to sell, you can still secure serious funding from strategic partners like we did with LinkedIn.

There is also a personal element that makes partnerships exciting. Most people fall into this type of role by accident, but the job is too good to leave its discovery up to chance.

Every day I get to meet new people who work at interesting companies. My network grew like crazy once I started this role. Part of my job is to network!

It's a cliché, but your network is your net worth. The longer you work in this field, the easier and the more fun it gets. Partnerships are also a senior and cross-functional role in most companies. This means you not only get to network with partners, you also get to work on projects with teams across your own business and paint the big picture together.

Now, don't get me wrong. Partnerships are not for the fainthearted. Whenever you get a third party involved, you give up control. This is uncomfortable, especially for CEOs and founders. They poured their blood, sweat, and tears into their business. Why should they now hand over the reins to someone else? It's like letting a stranger hold your baby! Terrifying! Yet if you can't delegate as a leader, you stand in the way of your company's growth. I hope this book will help you see how partnerships can be your unfair advantage and free your business from the shackles of wanting to do everything. All you need to do is learn how to identify and work with the right "strangers."

These skills will become more and more important in the future. Several trends have emerged that disrupt the traditional ways startups go to market. AI will make it easier than ever to spam prospects with emails, DMs, and fake phone calls. This will make outbound sales useless. At the same time, tools like ChatGPT will also drive the cost for new content down to zero. We already see the onset of a flood of AI-generated garbage content. Optimized for clicks and SEO, this might be the death of inbound marketing. Because of the impact AI will have on society, people are more concerned than ever about their data. Apple's updates to iOS made it a lot harder for Facebook and other advertisers to track you across the web. These companies won't be able to deliver the same results for your paid ads as they used to.

There is one source of information though that people will always rely on: trusted relationships. You can fake Amazon reviews with AI, but you can't fake a relationship. Trust takes a long time to build, which makes it hard to fake. This is why we will rely more and more on the influencers and companies we trust for recommendations. Jared Fuller calls this the shift from the "How" Economy to the "Who" Economy.[6] Partnerships allow you to surround your customers. They allow you to leverage trusted relationships to help customers make better decisions. Also known as "buy your product".

Now, I'm sure you already know that partnerships could be a game changer for your business. You might be a startup founder who slapped partnerships onto their pitch deck (I've been there). An entrepreneurial employee who wants to outsource their workload (I've done that). Or an account executive who wants to learn how to sell more deals together with partners (I've closed many). The real question is, "How do you build them?"

My goal for this book is to make partnerships as mainstream as sales or marketing. They are often talked about but rarely understood. To break this cycle, we need to explain all the core concepts in a way that anybody can understand.

You won't find any incomprehensible seven stage frameworks in this book. No quotations from Gartner or KPMG reports. I mean, when was the last time you read one of those? There's also no offer for a $2,000 course hidden at the end. Don't get me wrong. There are great frameworks, reports, and courses out there. But they are too complex to help us create the next generation of partnership leaders. There is also no secret agenda or sales pitch for expensive software.

I created this book because it is the book wish I had when I was in your shoes. My hope is it will help you create successful partnerships and avoid some of the mistakes I've made. And one day, maybe you decide to share your lessons and help us grow the partnerships community, too.

At this point, I also want to highlight that I did not write this book. I curated it. Yes, I will share a lot of my own lessons and failures. Yet a lot of this book is the summary of the work and stories of other partnership leaders. Strangers who became friends because they took the time to show me the ropes. Make sure to follow the people referenced in this book on LinkedIn. That's where many of them, including myself, share regular content about the cutting edge of our field. I also tagged their work in the endnotes so you can dive deeper into specific topics if you want to learn more.

My hope is that their stories will make this book more valuable because they extend far beyond my own limited experience. They are the ones who paved the way for my success in this field so I will make sure to give credit wherever I can.

In the next chapter, we will dive into the basics of partnerships like "When should you partner?" and "What types of partnerships are there?" After that, we'll follow up with four chapters. Each one will focus on an in-depth review of a specific type of partnership and how you can implement these partnerships at your startup.

Let's get into it!

CHAPTER 1:
PARTNERSHIP 101

"Strategy without tactics is the slowest route to victory, but tactics without strategy is the noise before the defeat."
—**Sun Tzu**

WHAT IS A PARTNERSHIP, ANYWAY?

Here's the biggest issue with partnerships: people think everything is a partnership! When you start a new partnership role, your email inbox will quickly turn into the "Other" folder of the company: Real Madrid wants us to be their t-shirt sponsor? Partnership. Random outbound sales message about a fringe payment service in the Philippines? Partnership. Annoying customer who asks about a "partnership" but really just wants a discount? Definitely a partnership.

One incident really drove this issue home for me. I came across a post in a startup forum where a founder asked the following:

> *"PARTNERSHIPS could be huge for us if we could figure out what that might look like. Have any of you done any GREAT partnerships that took your business to the next level?"*

Dozens of smart, intelligent people chimed in. Yet every single one of them talked about something else! Some talked about integrations. Others about posting on Instagram together. Another suggested sharing your email list with a partner. One person tried to cut through the confusion and suggested splitting partnerships into "commercial" and "non-commercial." It later turned out that "commercial partnership" was really just an awkward way to say "sales deal."

Why are people so confused about what a partnership is? You would think this is a basic question, but even seasoned veterans struggle to answer it. We often can't even agree on the terms to describe the type of partnership we are working on.

My best guess is there are two reasons for this confusion: One is that a partnership sounds like a win-win outcome. We all love those. So, people throw the word around loosely. For example, unsolicited sales messages will mention a "partnership" opportunity when in reality they want to sell you something. They are afraid to say this though, so they try to bait you into a call instead. A huge waste of time for everybody involved.

The other big issue is that partnerships look easy. How hard can it be to get two companies to work together? Because of this bias, a lot of people approach partnerships as a *cargo cult*.[2]

During World War II, the US military built airfields on small islands in the Pacific to supply their troops. To keep the local tribes happy, airplanes would often carry gifts for them. The locals loved these gifts. You can imagine their disappointment when the war ended. No more airplanes. No more gifts. The locals figured that under the right conditions, maybe the planes would land again. So, they cleared out air strips, lit them with torches at night, and even built air control huts with bamboo antennas. The operator inside wore headphones made of leaves.

This is what I see when a clueless startup founder emails me: "We would love to explore a partnership!" Leaf headphones. Just like the Pacific islanders, these people see other companies launch successful partnerships and want to do the same. But they don't understand the bigger picture and hidden principles that drive them.

Let's clear the fog once and for all. In the following chapters, we will unveil the secrets that separate the booms from the busts. The hits from the flops. The W's from the L's.

So, what is a partnership? I have poured over dozens of definitions. Mark Brigman, the founder of Partnernomics, created the closest thing I have found to a universal definition.[8] I shortened it somewhat to read:

A partnership is a relationship between two or more parties with the intent to create a competitive advantage.

There's a lot to unpack in this. The first thing is that partnerships are based on relationships. Companies do not partner with each other. People do. No matter if you work with a one-person startup or Microsoft with its 200,000+ employees. There is always at least one person on the other side who owns the relationship. This means your ability to build trust and work with strangers is a key ingredient for any successful partnership. Because trust can't be bought. It has to be earned, which makes it a valuable resource for any business.

The second is the creation of a competitive advantage. We all compete in the market. As companies, of course, but also as individuals. There's always a competitor who is after your customers. A colleague who mingles with management because they also want your promotion. A dude at the bar who has an eye on your crush. The goal of every partnership is to help you win. To sign on the customer. To get that promotion. To kiss the girl.

Partnerships come in many different shapes and flavors, but competitive advantages in business always manifest themselves in two ways: make money or save money. The best partners help you do both.

Let's take OpenAI's partnership with Microsoft as an example.[9] When the alliance was announced, the most obvious benefit to OpenAI was the $13 billion investment from Microsoft. An investment is not a partnership though. Money is generic so there is no competitive advantage in it. Look closer and you would realize that much of the $13 billion was in the form of cloud credits for Microsoft Azure data centers. That's a competitive advantage right there! It is expensive to train AI models. Access to huge amounts of compute power at lower than market rates gives you an edge over the competition.

Microsoft saved OpenAI money, but it got even better. ChatGPT, OpenAI's flagship product, would soon after be integrated into Microsoft's suite of products: Word, Excel, Powerpoint. You name it. Overnight, OpenAI had access to

Microsoft's 1.6 billion users. Microsoft, in return, rose to become the most valuable company in the world due to the hype around artificial intelligence and could offer cutting-edge features to all its users.[10] A complete step change for both companies. We will look at this partnership in more detail in chapter 6: Alliances.

This is the difference between a partnership and a sales deal. A sale does not create a competitive advantage because you don't have the same goal. One side lines their pockets while the other hopes their investment pays off. You don't share the risk. Even if you get a competitive edge from something you bought, your lead will evaporate in no time. Your competitor can just buy it, too.

For a partnership to succeed, both parties need to have the same idea of what it means to win. Your wing man might have a vested interest to help you marry your crush. He is a partner. But the bartender who pours you drinks in exchange for money? Not a partner. They don't care if you live happily ever after. All they want is to sell you drinks. I'd argue it's even bad for their business if you get married.

To frame this in business terms, partners need to support each other's business models. You already know how to make money from customers. So does your partner. How can you make more money together? The result of a partnership should always be bigger than the sum of its parts: 1 + 1 = 3.

Now that we know what a partnership is, let's circle back to the quote from the startup founder at the start of this chapter:

"PARTNERSHIPS could be huge for us if we could figure out what that might look like."

She is saying that partners could give her a huge competitive advantage. Makes sense. What she struggles with is that she doesn't know what types of partnerships would make the most sense for her business.

As I mentioned, even partnerships people get confused here. There are a lot of ways you could slice this question. Over the years, I have worked out a mental model that was quite accurate, but only after a conversation with Martin Scholz at PartnerXperience, did I realize why. The best way to distinguish partnerships is through the business function they support.[11]

Peter Caputa, CEO of Databox and one of the first account executives at HubSpot, explains: "Partnerships is not a team, but an overlay strategy for each department." What this means is that your partnership team doesn't have its own goals. It supports the goals of other departments at your company like marketing, customer support, sales, or product. I translated this into a graphic to visualize the five types of partnerships you might encounter with your startup:

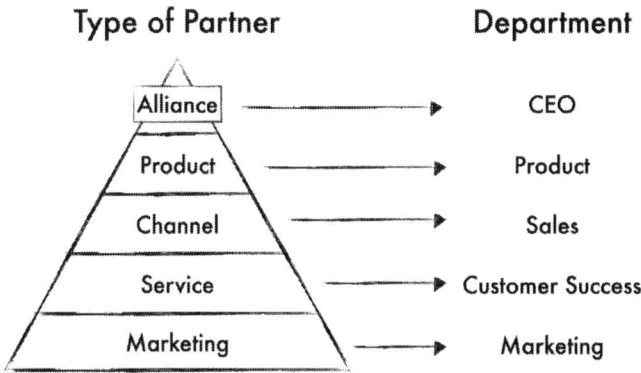

Fig. 1: The five types of partnerships and how they relate to each business function. Source: Franz-Josef Schrepf

Marketing Partnerships: These partners are an extension of your marketing team and should therefore align with the goals of this team. Marketing partnerships are what most people think of when they say partnership. I promote you to my customers and you do the same for me. No money changes hands, but there may be a small discount or kickback.

These partnerships are low-risk because it's easy to find out if they are worth the effort. Just tell your audience about the partner and see if they like their product. They are often low-risk, low-reward. It is easy to have a lot of them.

Service Partnerships: Any person or company that provides services around your product. These partners help you outsource manual, labor-intensive tasks like support, implementation, or fulfillment. The goals of these partners should align with your customer success (CS) team. It takes time to enable service partners and their teams, so you'll probably have fewer of them. This increases the risk of choosing the wrong partners. On the flip side, because these partners do invest time into learning your tool they are more committed to the partnership and can also provide more value to your customers.

Channel Partnerships: Channel partners are companies that work with manufacturers or producers to sell their products on their behalf. The main goal of these partnerships is to extend the reach of your sales team. In the past, all resellers did was distribute your product. Like when you got your CDs onto the shelves of a Radio Shack. The internet completely disrupted this business model. Today, most partners in this category are *value-added resellers (VARs)*. VARs bundle your product with their own services and products, offering them as a comprehensive package deal.

Product Partnerships: These are other tech companies who usually integrate with your software. An integration is not a partnership though. Justin Zimmerman at Partner Playbooks was so upset about people confusing the two, he even made it his tagline: "Integrations ≠ Partnerships."[12] That's because your product team can often build an integration all by themselves. All they need is a public API. A product partnership is the go-to-market wrapper around your integration or joint customer workflows. It's expensive to build integrations, which makes these partnerships higher risk than the other types. But your joint solution might be worth a lot more money to your customers. It also means that you won't be able to onboard as many of them. At Hopin we had hundreds of service and channel partners, but only 50 integrations.

Alliances: The holy grail of partnerships. The sumos. The big whales. While most partners will only add incremental growth to your business, alliances lead to exponential growth.[13] For example, Microsoft gave OpenAI access to 16 times the number of customers they already had.

The main difference here is the depth of the partnership. Alliances are multi-threaded.[14] They are a combination of all the different types of partnerships we mentioned above. On top of that, your goal is to also "win" the partner's ecosystem. To work with all the marketing, service, channel, and product partners that surround your alliance partner.

Alliances are often also called *strategic partnerships* or *strategic alliances*. That's because an alliance can shift your entire business and even the market you operate in. They are "bet the company" type decisions. These types of partnerships often require all the resources of your company and create a heavy reliance on the alliance partner. For this reason, alliances cannot be owned by a department. The CEO has to own these decisions. She has to make sure all teams pull in the same direction. Most startups will struggle to even do one alliance well, so focus is key. Choose wisely.

These are the five main types of partnerships you will encounter as a startup. We will discuss each one of them in more detail later in the book. There are other things that people also call a "partnership."[15] But if you probe them, you will realize that they usually fall into one of these five buckets. Or they are something a startup would not do. Like joint ventures. I mean, come on! You should focus on your own venture first!

My hope is that this breakdown has cleared some of the confusion. We discussed what a partnership is. How they relate to each department in your organization. And what types of partnerships exist. Next time somebody asks you how partnerships can help their business, at minimum you should be able to show them this graphic and ask: "What type of partners are you looking for?"

We'll go into more detail on each of the five buckets in later chapters. For now, I want to point out three additional features of this graphic:

First, you can see that each bucket is represented by a slimmer banner than the previous one. This is by design. Marketing partnerships require the least amount of effort, so you can have a lot of them. Just fire off some social media posts and call it a day. Alliances are the most resource intensive, you'll likely only have one of them at a time. This means that your risk of failure is much more concentrated. If a marketing partner messes up, you just move on. At most there will be only minor damage. The wrong alliance partner can kill your business.

On the flip side, higher risks correlate with higher rewards. A marketing partner might send you some new customers. But they won't change the trajectory of your entire business like an alliance. If they did, they probably wouldn't be a marketing partner. If a marketing partner shovels customer leads to you like no tomorrow, you would invest in that partner. You would train their team. Make it easier for them to sell. Integrate with their workflows. Engage all of their partners. They would become an alliance partner. Which brings me to my next point.

The five types of partnerships often stack on top of each other. In my experience, partnerships often progress from one rung of the pyramid to another. We call this the *crawl, walk, run approach*. If you like the look of a partner, you might strike up a conversation with their audience first. A casual marketing partnership. Maybe a blog post or a webinar. Low risk, low effort, no real commitment yet. All cool and easy.

If you see it works, you might decide to train their team on how to use your platform. Just so they can help any joint customers who might have questions, Maybe the partners' team starts to recommend your tool, so you explore how you could sell together. Wow, you have so many joint customers now! That's when you decide to double down and integrate your two products, so they work better together. Finally, you look around and see that there is a whole ecosystem around your partner. So, you decide to partner with them, too. You have now officially formed an alliance.

When you take this approach, something curious will happen. You might decide that you formed an alliance with a partner, but they think you just have another marketing partnership. Eric Chan, former head of global partnerships at revenue management platform Chargebee, pointed out that partnerships are often not symmetrical and equitable. If your startup wants to partner with Google, you will need to put in an alliance level effort. All-hands-on-deck. But the Google team? They might get away with an email and a blog post to keep you happy. You are only one of many partners until you have proven your value.

WHY DO MOST PARTNERSHIPS FAIL?

Like marriage, the divorce rate among partners is sky high. So, why do most partnerships fail? Throughout my career, I had far more misses than wins. If you ever tried to form a partnership before, chances are it didn't go well either. So, before we dig deeper into the theory, I want to host a pre-mortem.

If you work in software, you probably know what a post-mortem is. It is the dreadful meeting where you discuss what went wrong, why your team failed, and how to do better next time. The issue with these is that by the time you host the meeting you have already failed. Instead, our founders at StreamYard host a weekly pre-mortem to answer the question: "What could cause us to fail?" Then we try our best to not let these things happen. I highly recommend you host a session like this with your partners as well to get on the same page.

There are plenty of reasons why different types of partnerships fail: exclusivity clauses, culture fit, bankruptcy, lack of leadership buy-in, plain simple incompetence. The list goes on and we'll discuss many of these in detail later. However, after hundreds of partnerships and even more conversations with other partnership leaders, I learned that there seem to be two key reasons for failure: incentives and time.

Cory Snyder captured this idea in a webinar: "All partnerships fail because you don't understand the incentives that drive the people around you."[16] Every partnership involves at least three parties: your company, the partner company, and your joint customer. The main reason why these partnerships fail is because at least one of these groups thinks there isn't enough in it for them. I call this the Partnership Value Triangle.

```
        Customer
       /\
      /  \
     /    \
   Partner ←→ Company
```

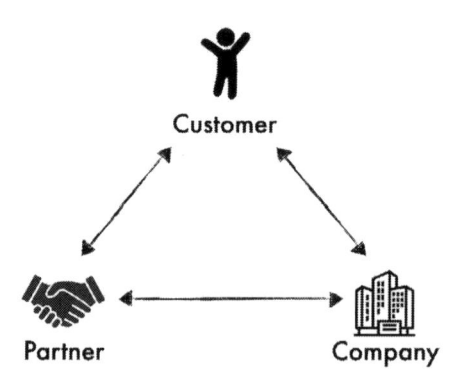

Fig. 2: The Partnership Value Triangle. Source: Franz-Josef Schrepf

The most common issue with incentives is that you or your leadership team got starstruck by a shiny brand. This happened to me when our CEO had dinner with the founder of a large, publicly traded company. He arranged for me to be introduced to their product and partnerships team. I was over the moon! I had chased their team for months and now we were all on a call. Excitement was high. They loved our pitch and roped more people into the conversation. At the peak, more than 10 employees of their company got involved.

A few weeks later though, the partnership unraveled. Why? Because their main incentive was to appease their CEO. Once he shifted his attention to a new project, his team dropped the ball and went back to other projects which they thought were higher impact.

Be aware of *buddyware*, a partnership that was only started because the CEOs or partnership leaders of both companies want to trade favors. Any partnership like this is dead on arrival. That's because your CEO is not your boss. The customer is your boss. They are the ones who decide whether a partnership is successful. Leadership teams are often too far removed from the front lines to really appreciate what customers want. Fortunately, there is a simple fix to this problem: talk to your customers.

Another issue with incentives arises when you and your customers would get a lot of value out of a partnership, but your partner doesn't. This often happens when the cost of partnering is too high (e.g., you need to build an integration which can take months) or the upside for the partner is too low. A $100,000 deal might be a lot of money to you, but for Google it barely covers the Kombucha budget. For one office. For one flavor.

This is an issue because if there is not enough upside for any of the three parties, they will not invest in the partnership. They might still agree to do it, but it will be a half-hearted yes. Like when you agree to help your friend move house, face instant regret, and then spend all Saturday thinking how you can get out of this commitment. While the customer is your boss, a partnership still needs to make sense for all parties involved. To cover your blind spots, Chris Lavoie recommends you start with the customer's incentive, then the partner's, and finally your own.[17]

If you don't put your customer first, you might also fall into what Greg Portnoy calls a *Barney Partnership*.[18] Like the big purple dinosaur Barney, you and your partner hold hands during meetings, sing songs about your joint value proposition and all the money you'll make, and share how much you love each other. You just can't wait to tell the world all about it. Until the market slaps you in the face and pulls you back into reality. Customers don't care if you love a partner. They have to love them, too.

The Partnerships Value Triangle can help set you up for success or troubleshoot if your partnership efforts have stalled. One big mistake here is to fill in the blanks on behalf of your partners and customers. This might come as a shock to any introvert, but you have to talk to them. Ask your partner and customers questions like:

- "Why did you buy into this partnership?"
- "Why are partners important to you and your business?"
- "How do partners impact your company?"
- "Who on your team should we involve in this decision?"

This process may look simple, but what makes it complex is that behind each group is a team of people who can all have different incentives. You and your marketing team might love a big-name partner, but that doesn't matter if your product team has a tight deadline for an important feature. Joe Rice, former head of developer platform at Twitter, put it like this: "Partnerships are as much about internal selling as they are about external selling."[19] Don't be afraid to say no or hold off until you are sure all parties are fully aligned.

We also have the issue that incentives will change over time. In sales, we have a saying: "Time kills deals." In fact, time kills everything in business. That's because your job as a startup is to identify and exploit opportunities faster than your competitors.

Opportunities are, by definition, time sensitive. A customer has a problem and they need someone to fix it. If you wait too long, either a competitor will have filled the gap, or the problem goes away. Maybe because the customer's company died. That's right. Your inaction killed your customer. This is why I start every follow-up meeting with the question: "What changed?" And I still get it wrong.

A while back I wanted to partner with another industry giant. They were my white whale. After months of cold outreach and warm intros, I finally managed to get their head of partnerships on a call. I validated his pain points and then pitched him on a partnership. He was over the moon! He even offered to launch the partnerships as part of an exclusive event they were hosting at their HQ in four months. 75 of their top customers would be there. I thought we had hit the jackpot.

During the preparation for the event, cracks started to form. The head of partnerships handed off the project to one of his team members. This junior partner manager then flagged that she was not aware of the event being part of a larger partnership discussion. Soon after we were told that we would not be part of the main agenda of the event but could still attend. Finally, we were uninvited. To top things off, the partner manager also quit her job.

What happened? I had built up enough trust with the partner manager to ask her this question. She was on the way out anyway, so she shared that there had been several internal changes. The writing was on the wall that there would be layoffs, so a lot of team members left. The ones who stayed couldn't take on all leftover projects, so they narrowed their focus on a few top priority initiatives. As a new partner, this did not include us.

Time killed this deal. Months of work down the drain. If we had moved faster, we might have been able to show results from our partnership that would have convinced their team to keep us on.

Bernie Brenner, the founder of TrueCar, drove this lesson home for me: "[In partnerships] it's never, ever OK, unless there's some catastrophe, to just go, 'Well, we just have to sit and wait.'"[20] A key part of partnerships is to get your ducks in a row so you can strike when the timing is right. And it all starts with the right partner strategy.

YOUR BUILD, BUY, PARTNER STRATEGY

The word "strategy" is even more often abused than "partnerships." We have all sat through hour long strategy sessions and looked at 20-page strategy documents only to be none the wiser. What are our company and teams actually supposed to do? What is a strategy?

Strategy is a choice. You have to choose where to play and how to win.[21] Every company and partnerships team has a limited number of resources. You can't play in every arena or you'll be spread too thin. Your competitors with more discipline and focus will always see this as an open invitation to swoop in and crush you. So, the goal of your strategy has to be to figure out where you should apply your resources to maximize your chance of success.

This sounds an awful lot like a business strategy, not a partner strategy. That's because it is. As Jared Fuller says, "Partnerships is not a department, it's a strategy for every department."[22]

Yes, you might be the head of the partnership department. But the biggest mistake you can make is to come up with a partnership strategy all by yourself. You can't implement a partnership on your own. All team members, from product to sales to support, need to work together to make a partnership work.

These teams have a lot of other stuff on their plate. To incentivize them to engage with you, every partnership needs to directly impact the metrics they are measured on. So, the goals of your partnerships team need to be the same as the goals of the departments you need to work with. Marketing partnerships need to align closely with the goals of the marketing team. Product partnerships with the product team. And so on.

This is what Peter Caputa means when he says that partnerships are "an overlay strategy for all departments." They are a core piece of your company strategy and help every team win.

The simplest way to visualize partnerships as part of your company strategy and the strategy of each department is the *build, buy, partner matrix*.[23]

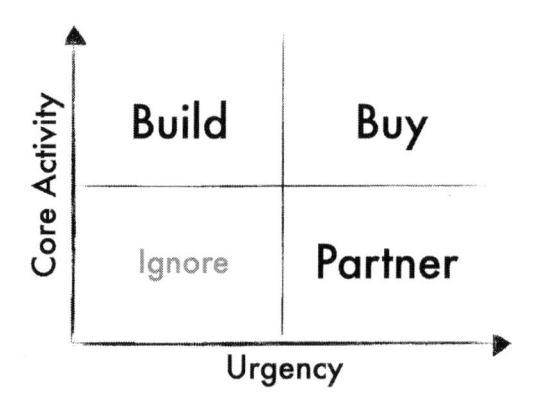

Fig. 3: The Build, Buy, Partner Matrix. Source: Franz-Josef Schrepf

Imagine your customers ask your startup or department to add a new capability to your product or service offering. You will have to decide whether this is a space you want to play in. These types of decisions depend on two factors: Is this capability a core activity for our business and how urgently do we need it?

Core activities are capabilities that increase the sustainable competitive advantage of a company. They are things you need to be good at to create value for your customers in a way that is hard to replicate for competitors.[24] Urgency describes how much time pressure there is for your company to add this capability right now. Based on these inputs, you can take four possible actions:

Build: If you decide that a feature or service is core to your business, you should bring it in-house. These core activities make up the unique selling points of your business, so you need to guard them at all costs. Most startup founders have a bias to build things themselves because this gives them complete control over the project roadmap and ownership of the intellectual property (IP). The issue is that it often takes a long time to build things from scratch and there is a lot of execution risk if you decide to enter a new space which you don't understand.

Buy: A faster way to bring capabilities in-house is to buy them. This often refers to buying the whole company. But startups tend to be broke, so you can also just buy their products or services as a customer. That way you have access to a team with expertise and a product that, hopefully, works and has been tested in the market. However, this is often the most expensive option and there can be hidden issues like integration costs or incompatible company cultures that could cause trouble down the line.

Partner: This is usually the least expensive and fastest option to add capabilities to your company offering. Partners already know how to offer the feature or task you need so all you need to do is plug them in. You effectively split the risks and rewards of adding this capability between you and your partner. This makes partnerships a great test bed for capabilities if you are not sure whether you really need them or should bring them in-house.

Ignore: If a feature or service is not core to your business and not urgent, why are we even talking about it? You have bigger fish to fry. Realistically, this is where most requests and ideas end up. Strategy is more about the things you don't do than what you actually decide to do.

Technically, there's a fifth option: invest. It's when you dull out cash to your partners to show how committed you are to the partnerships and to buy a stake in their hopefully successful business. It's a great way to get more skin in the game. But since this is a book for startups, I recommend that you hold on to your spare change. You'll need it. Investments make most sense for large companies with time horizons longer than the entire life of your startup.

The process where you decide if and how to add capabilities to your company's offering to satisfy customer needs is called *business development.* You "develop" the business and chart a path for its future growth. But like partnerships, this term gets abused a lot. These days, people often say business development when they mean sales. Oh well.

Here is a simple example of what this process looks like in action: our core business at Hopin was to host virtual events for clients. Imagine a mix of a webinar, zoom calls, and chat roulette for big online events with thousands of people.

Because these events were online, it was easy to attract an international audience. This meant that event organizers wanted to offer content in multiple languages. The ability to add interpretation services to our platform was urgent for us because we may lose a lot of customers to a competitor if they decided to offer this feature. But we are not a translation company. We do not have interpreters on our staff. We do not have expertise in interpretation and internationalization of content. So we partnered and integrated with the top platforms our customers wanted to use for this service.

I learned the hard way how important it is to defend your core capabilities, though. One customer insisted on a specific set of business networking features for their event. This customer was important to us, but there was no way we could build what they asked for in time for their event. The customer then went out and found a company they wanted us to integrate with. That's when things went south.

The company they found was a small competitor of ours. Never partner with competitors. Partnerships are about trust. How can you trust someone who wants to take your business? Worst of all, the competitor knew we were in a pickle and wanted us to pay for the integration on top of the money they got from the customer. Remember what people who push for win-lose outcomes are called?

After weeks of negotiations, we arrived at an agreement and built the integration. Yet event attendees hated it. Networking was a core part of the experience, but the integration felt clunky and confusing. The customer wasn't happy either and terminated their contract after the event.

Several months later I learned that the competitor not only trash-talked us to the customer behind our back, they also built features the event organizer wanted and hosted the entire event for the customer the following year. In hindsight, it was obvious. We introduced a high-value customer to a competitor and they stole them. Ouch.

The business development process requires discipline and selfless leadership. We knew that networking was core to our business. If we couldn't build or buy this capability, the right move would have been to explain this to the customer. We might have still lost them to the same competitor, but at least there wouldn't have been the sting of countless hours of our time and energy wasted on a partnership that resulted in chaos.

Another issue are biases within each team. Product wants to build, Corporate Development wants to buy, and Partnerships have a partner hammer that makes everything look like a partner nail. As Scott Pollack, former VP of business development at WeWork, says, "The onus is really on you, as a partner leader, to demonstrate over time that you are a true steward of value for the company."[25]

HOW TO FIND PARTNERSHIP OPPORTUNITIES?

Now that we understand the build, buy, partner framework, the next question is "how do we come up with ideas for features or services to add in those boxes?" As you can see from my examples above, most of the time these ideas will come to you in the form of customer requests. The timeline and importance of the customer to your startup give you a good idea of the urgency of the request. However, they do not give you a sense of whether a feature is core to your business. Customer feedback is also often short-term oriented and creates blind spots where long-term risks creep up on you until it is too late. For instance, when the market for virtual events evaporated once COVID restrictions were removed. Our event organizer customers were convinced that virtual events would be the new normal. Turns out their event attendees disagreed.

One helpful exercise to understand your core activities and spot overall market trends is a classic business school framework called SWOT analysis.[26] SWOT stands for strengths, weaknesses, opportunities, and threats. The goal of this framework is to map out your competitive position based on internal factors—strengths and weaknesses, and external market forces—opportunities and threats.

	Helpful	Harmful
Internal	Strength	Weakness
External	Opportunity	Threat

Fig. 4: SWOT Analysis.

There are dozens of other frameworks you could use to come up with ideas, too. The reason why I prefer this one is its simplicity and how well it integrates into the business development process: internal factors help you determine whether something is a core activity. External factors help you determine the urgency with which you need to add this activity.

This is one of the big mistakes I made early in my partnerships career. I would identify a weakness which we could address with a partner, like translation services, and a strength we could offer in exchange, like our large audience of potential customers. Then I showed how this partnership would provide value to our joint customers— the classic partner value triangle we discussed before.

This type of pitch worked well for small partners who wanted to work with us because we were the bigger fish. But it fell on deaf ears with large partners because I missed a crucial piece: urgency. I forgot to put my pitch into the context of the wider market. Why should we partner right now? What opportunities or threats do both of our businesses face? Once I included these external factors into my pitch, my success rate improved dramatically.

One example of this framework in action is Adobe's attempted acquisition of Figma for $20 billion in 2022.[27] Adobe was the market leader in software for creatives. However, a mega trend posed a serious threat to their business: collaborative, browser-based software. Designers don't want to download files each time they make a change, send them to their colleagues for review, and then piece together loose bits of feedback. They want everything in the cloud where they can work on their designs together with the team.

New startups rushed in to fill the gap and steal Adobe's customers. The most imminent threat was Figma, a collaborative design tool, which became the de facto standard in the industry. Adobe realized that cloud-based design in your browser was the future and core to their business. But they lagged so far behind Figma that there was no way to build a competitive solution. Figma knew this and used it to their advantage during negotiations to achieve a $20 billion price tag on $400 million annual recurring revenue (ARR), a 50x revenue multiple which is incredible. Unfortunately, the deal was blocked by regulators since they deemed it anti-competitive.

Throughout this exercise, you will be tempted to make assumptions and fill in the blanks for your partners and customers. As Marco De Paulis, director of partnerships at e-commerce startup Loop, always says: "Don't predict, ask!"[28]

One of Adobe's weaknesses was their size. They are so big and dominant in the market that regulators will pay close attention to their transactions. Their team made the assumption that this would not be an issue and paid the price. Regulators won't be an issue for you, but when in doubt always verify your assumptions with your internal stakeholders, partners, and customers.

Okay, let's take a step back. Build, buy, partner and SWOT. Basically, two 2x2 graphics. Can a strategy really be this simple? Will people think you're serious if you don't rock up to the meeting with a 20-page document and complicated charts? Glad you asked, let me tell you a quick story:

It is March 1942 and US president Franklin Delano Roosevelt (FDR) faces the legitimate threat of losing World War II to Nazi Germany and Japan. The axis powers had a string of victories and it seemed like the tides of history were in their favor. One day, during a conversation with his commanding general, FDR grabbed a cocktail napkin and scribbled on it a three-point action plan: hold four key territories, attack Japan, and attack France. The general took it back to the Pentagon where it remained a classified key pillar of the allied war effort for years. While the plan seemed basic, it gave the US military leadership the clarity and focus they needed to persevere. You can find an image of the napkin online.[29]

Did FDR come up with a winning strategy on a whim? No. It's more likely that FDR consulted for countless hours with his generals and read hundreds of pages of intelligence reports. He then summarized all this information into three simple bullet points. Any member of the US military, regardless of their rank, could understand and execute this strategy. So yes, you can have your 20-page strategy document, excel sheets with 10,000 rows, and countless hours of conversations with customers to inform your partner strategy. But you need to be able to explain it in a way that is simple enough for everybody on your team to understand and buy into it. If FDR can win WWII with a napkin, you can put your partner strategy on one slide.

IDEAL PARTNER PROFILES:
THE 4 CS OF PARTNERSHIPS

Now that we know there is an opportunity to fill a gap in your offering, a validated customer need, and a rough idea for the partnership incentives, the big question is: Who do we partner with?

In his book *The Mom Test*, Rob Fitzpatrick shares that: "Startups don't starve, they drown."[30] Partnerships are like mini-startups, which means the risk here is not that you won't have enough potential partners. You will probably have too many.

Nelson Wang, head of worldwide partnerships at Airtable, learned this lesson the hard way. Back in 2013, he was hired to build out the partner program at Box, a cloud storage and collaboration tool for enterprises. He went to work and recruited 700 partners (!!!) into his program.[31] He admitted that in hindsight there were way too many partners compared to their customer needs and the goals they were trying to achieve. So he created a framework to filter for the right partners for his program. Soon after, the revenue generated by his program exploded from zero to $100 million+. He then replicated his success at four more companies. The framework he created is called the 4Cs of partnerships: customers, capabilities, capacity, and commitment.[32]

Customers: How many shared customers do you have? The biggest mistake I and countless other partnership leaders have made is that we assumed we had to do research to find the right partners. Several books and blogs claim that the best way to find partners is to read whitepapers and industry reports by Gartner. Some also suggest scouring software review sites like G2 for the Top 100 tools you could partner with. All of this is bad advice for one simple reason: What do these people know about your customers? Nothing.

Your goal at this stage is to find *partner-market-fit*. This means you want to figure out who your customers want to work with. Again, don't predict. Ask. Let your customers tell you how they currently solve the problem that you have identified in your build, buy, partner framework. What tools and workflows do they use? Who provides services to them? Which influencers have their attention and give them advice? Over time you will get a clear picture of the sphere of influence around your customers:

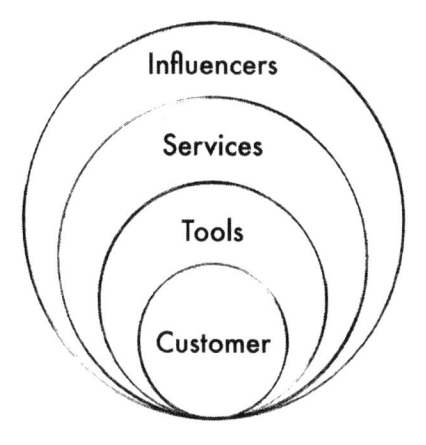

Fig. 5: Your Customer's Ecosystem and Circles of Influence.
Source: Franz-Josef Schrepf

Your customer needs to be at the center of every partner decision you make. The customer is your boss. They decide whether you succeed or not. One step further are the tools and workflows your customer uses. I bet they spent a lot of time and money figuring out their processes, so they won't rip and replace them just for you. You need to integrate with those workflows. The further out you move, the less critical these partners become to your customer. A recommendation from a trusted friend or influencer is great. But if the tool only works with Gmail and you use Outlook for your emails, you still won't buy it.

To supplement these interviews, I also like to live like my customers. When we acquired StreamYard, I decided to use our tool and start my own live show. I realized how easy it is to get obsessed about every aspect of your show. I quickly learned who the key influencers were because I wanted to watch their content. Then I tested the products they recommended and built workflows around them. This gave me an edge when I had to evaluate whether our customers would want to engage with one of these partners.

Another way to discover partners is to ask your customer-facing teams. Most companies already have several partners in their orbit, they just don't know it. I call this your *Shadow Partner Program*. When we wanted to build our event agencies program at Hopin, I offhandedly mentioned the idea to one of our customer success managers (CSMs). She lit up and said: "Oh you should talk to Franco and Tina!" Turns out two of her customers were event agencies. They worked a lot together and became friends with the CSM. Now, every time somebody asked her for help with their event setup or video production services, she pointed them to those two agencies.

There were over a dozen agencies like this. What a low hanging fruit! These informal relationships were the ideal starting point for our partner program because the agencies already knew how to use our software and had several shared customers. All we had to do was talk to them, understand what they needed from us, and formalize the partnership. The main takeaway here is that a lot of partnerships aren't built, they are uncovered. You just have to listen to what your customers and partners want.

For this reason, I always say that your first partners won't be an inbound lead. Like a strange LinkedIn request from someone who is "eager to explore ways we can collaborate for mutual success." Your CEO will forward you all the random emails he gets from companies that want to partner. Maybe you receive dozens of requests from that partnership intake form you put on your website. None of these things matter unless those companies can prove that they understand your customers the way you do. And most of them can't even spell the name of your company correctly. There are, of course, other ways to find partners which we will discuss in later chapters.

Capabilities: Can the partner solve a customer problem you identified as part of your build, buy, partner strategy? This one might seem obvious, but I have fallen on my face here, too. In 2021, Web3 and crypto were all the rage. A lot of our customers wanted to incorporate some form of NFTs or crypto payments into their events. The issue was that none of them knew how or what they wanted. So I went out and did research. Classic mistake.

We found a partner who offered customers the option to pay with crypto (cool) and turn their tickets into NFTs (very cool). We spent months on the integration. Yet on launch day nobody wanted to use it. Turns out our customers did not want to use a product that lacked a SOC2 security certification. This type of audit can take years to obtain which is hard to do if your crypto startup was founded four months ago in your mom's basement.

In short, the partner was not ready for prime time. This was my mistake. I did not spend enough time with customers to really understand what capabilities they needed, like security certifications.

Capacity: Can your partner deliver at the scale you need? This is one of the most frequent reasons why we shut down partner conversations. At StreamYard, we often get approached by small live streaming platforms with a variation of this pitch: "We are the #1 live shopping platform in Europe. A lot of our customers use the StreamYard studio to produce live streams on our platform so we would love to explore a partnership. We have already identified nine customers who are asking for it."

The pitch itself is not bad. The partner does play in a relevant market. There would be value in the integration. And they have shared customers. All this is great. But as a company with millions of users, we need bigger opportunities. There is little incentive for us to work with them unless they have tens of thousands of other customers on top of the nine they told me about.

The inverse can also be true. For the Hopin agency program, we intentionally worked with smaller partners at the start. Our own team was only 80 people and virtual events were brand new. We wanted to personally train each team member of our partner agencies on how to service our platform. We then gathered their feedback on our certification process so we could scale the program later.

Small partners had the patience to build with us. The handful of leads we sent them were enough to keep them afloat and grow their business. Large, global agencies with hundreds of employees would have spelled disaster. We either would have not met their expectations, or they would have overwhelmed us with support requests from all their employees. Only when we were sure we could handle these large partners did we onboard them.

Commitment: How much does the partner want to work with you now and in the future? Tai Rattigan, former global head of partnerships at analytics scaleup Amplitude, shared that there is a secret ingredient to make sure your partner stays committed: Find something in their core business that benefits from your business and makes it easier to sell together.[33]

Tai saw this firsthand with one of their partners, the customer engagement platform Braze. Amplitude's analytics gave customers deep visibility into their customer's behavior across their entire journey. The insights itself were helpful, but what supercharged them was the ability to make real time updates to the customer's digital experience, like email or in-app messages, with Braze.

The two tools combined provided amazing customer value and the integration was a strong differentiator for Braze. It made their product much easier to sell, so their sales team was motivated to be a great referral partner for Amplitude. Hype and referral fees will only get you so far. To get your partner to commit for the long run, you need to become a fundamental part of their business.

To sum it up, here are the four questions you need to ask your partners to measure *partner-market-fit* with the 4C's framework:

1. **Customers:** How many shared customers do you have?
2. **Capabilities:** Can the partner solve a customer problem you identified as part of your build, buy, partner strategy?
3. **Capacity:** Can your partner deliver at the scale you need?
4. **Commitment:** How much does the partner want to work with you now and in the future?

This might sound like a lot to consider, but it will get easier. Over time, a pattern will emerge on what partners work best for your company. This is called an *ideal partner profile (IPP)*. It is similar to the ideal customer profile (ICP) your startup might already have. The biggest mistakes founders make with their ICP and IPP is that they don't base them in reality.

In the past we made the mistake of creating generic ICPs: Thomas, 28 years old, loves to host events. These aren't helpful. Instead, now we use actual customers and partners as examples for our ideal profiles. One of the agency owners we worked with, Enrico, grew his agency from 10 to 40 people as a result of our partnership. So instead of some vague IPP description we ask: "Could this partner be another Enrico?" This approach works because it captures a lot more nuance than a fictional character. Our team knows Enrico, so they can notice patterns that we couldn't capture in a generic profile.

Now a word of warning: The more you learn how to filter partners with the 4Cs and your IPP, the more often you will have to say "no." I like to compare partnerships to the role of a venture capitalist (VC). You will listen to a lot of pitches, but you can't allocate resources to all of them. 95% will never make it to the next stage.

A lot of people struggle with this. Yet at some point in my career, I had wasted enough people's time to realize that you don't do anybody a favor if you drag your feet or lead them on. Don't try to be nice, but be kind. Nice people hide behind fake smiles and create artificial harmony. Kind people tell you the truth so you can improve or move onto something else.

One time, I pursued a large partner for months. Finally, they agreed to jump on a call with me to make my relentless emails stop. They again said no, but also explained their own build, buy, partner rationale to me over the next thirty minutes. Of course, it wasn't the outcome I wanted, but we had a great discussion, and I was very impressed with my counterpart. She made me see that my time is definitely better spent somewhere else, and I appreciated that.

A "no" opens up the door to a thousand other opportunities. With a "yes" you commit to one path and shut out everything else. Choose wisely.

WHEN SHOULD YOU INVEST IN PARTNERSHIPS?
We talked a lot about how shared customers are one of the most important ingredients of any successful partnership. I am sure this made some readers uncomfortable. What if you don't have any customers yet, let alone shared ones? Should you still invest in partnerships?

This is for sure the most controversial chapter. I've debated this topic with dozens of partnership leaders and surveyed the community.[34] In a recent poll, 56% of partnership leaders responded that startups should invest in partnerships from day one. I think they are wrong. And because I don't mind starting a war, let me tell you why.

Partnerships should always be rooted in what your customers want. This is impossible to do if you don't know who your customers are. We made this painful mistake with our first startup. Yes, we had that big shiny partnership with Google's AMP team. Yes, we got hundreds of thousands of people who used our product. But we had no idea who our ideal customer was.

These people came from all walks of life. They all wanted different things. Their feedback pulled us in all sorts of directions. It felt impossible to focus on one type of customer since there were so many of them. But because we tried to serve everybody, we served nobody well. None of these users stuck around. I felt like I had to watch sand run through my fingers.

Don't pour rocket fuel in an engine that isn't ready for takeoff. As we mentioned in the beginning, partners support each other's business models. But how can they do this if you don't know what your business model is? If you don't know how to make money in a repeatable way?

The same goes for your other C's: capabilities, capacity, and commitment. If you have not figured out your core activities yet, you don't fit into a partner's build, buy, partner strategy. You need to build your own strengths first. In the same vein, partnerships are not a sprint, they're a marathon. You wouldn't commit to a marathon without getting in your training runs first?

Also, your biggest asset as a startup is flexibility. Yet if two companies decide to partner, they commit to a course. We made this mistake once with a new product we built at Hopin. Our customers wanted a lighter-weight version of our virtual events platform. Like a Zoom call, but more fun and engaging. One of our teams built a prototype and of course got excited about all the potential partnership opportunities they found. The most obvious ones were with meeting scheduling tools. This would allow users to book meetings and host them on our tool. Makes sense. I also got swept away by the team's excitement.

I soon developed a pitch for a potential partner and courted them. After several months we finally had an integration and a joint go-to-market strategy in place. That's when our team decided that they wanted to go after a different type of customer. The partnership was no longer needed. Not only did we waste months of effort. We also incurred what we in partnerships call *relationship debt*. We burnt a bridge with this partner, which made them less likely to work with us in the future. Worse, word travels fast. This incident also decreased our chances of working with other partners. Our reputation took a big hit.

This is why I don't think you should partner from day one. Your job as an early-stage startup is to find your own customers and core activities first. Everything else is a distraction. Cristina Cordova, former head of partnerships at Notion, even says: "Don't do partnerships, if possible.[35]" That's because partnerships create dependencies that tie you down. You want to stay flexible at the start and give yourself room to maneuver.

Alex Glenn, CEO of Partnerhub, also agrees: "To me, the 56% of respondents who said "Day one" were clicking that option for their own job security."[36] When you have a partnership hammer, everything looks like a partnership nail. The irony is that with this approach you shoot yourself in the foot. If your company isn't ready for partnerships yet, you will fail. Then you lose your job, and the startup will be hesitant to invest when the time is right.

So, when should you invest in partnerships? I talked about this with Jay LeBoeuf, former head of business development at Descript, on my podcast:

> *"I can see how someone would say you should invest in partnerships at day one if you think partners will be an important way to reach your audience. If that is your channel, maybe you want to start building those relationships early. But day one for most startups, you have no product-market-fit. You barely have a product. [...] You have convinced your friends, family, and maybe a few investors that you can do this, but you are not ready to scale."*[37]

The last part is crucial: Are you ready to scale? Marc Andreessen, investor at the venture capital fund a16z and inventor of the internet browser, thinks of startups in two stages: before and after product-market-fit (PMF). He defines PMF as "being in a good market with a product that can satisfy this market."[38] It's when you know that customers want your product.

This is all a bit vague though. How do you know if you have PMF? In his book *Hacking Growth,* Sean Ellis describes a simple test. If over 40% of your users say they would be "very disappointed" if they could no longer use your product, it's a strong indicator of PMF.[39] You can often see the moment companies hit PMF in their user growth chart and how it relates to the investment they receive from VCs:

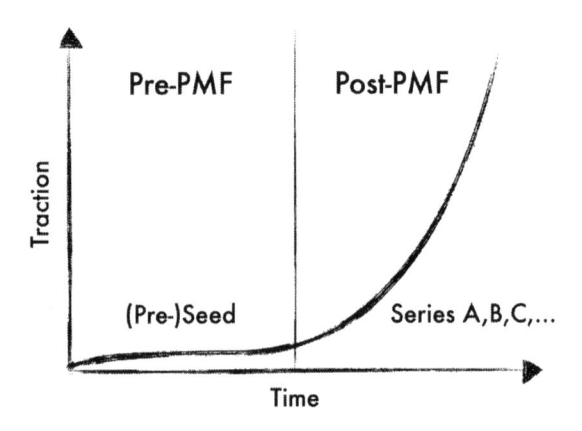

Fig. 6: The startup maturity and fundraising life cycle.

The first half of this chart, the pre-seed and seed stages, are focused on customer discovery. This is your day one. Your goal is to figure out what problem customers have and how to build a solution that they want. This is the time when you figure out your own core activities. Most startups will never make it past this stage. The good news is that during this time you will face little meaningful competition. Your market is not validated yet, so competitors will find it too risky to jump in. The same counts for partners. As Joe Rice puts it: "If you don't have product-market-fit, no sane partner would want to spend time with you." And I don't recommend you partner with the insane.[40]

All this changes once you find product-market-fit. The moment you have proven that customers want your solution, competitors will take note. Your goal now is to onboard as many customers as possible before anybody else sweeps them up. This is the land-grab phase. Now that it is less risky, VCs will also be happy to pour more cash into your startup. Funding rounds are now called series A, B, C etc., because their single purpose is to help you scale what works.[41]

You built the rocket engine, now you just need more fuel to reach *escape velocity*—when you are too fast and far ahead for your competitors to ever catch up to you. Partners can be your unfair advantage as you scale. So the right time to invest should be between the seed and Series A stage, when you have enough proof that customers want your product.

Not all partnership people agree with this approach. Jared Fuller shared that "pros win by being precise."[42] They need to know not just who their customer is, but also who surrounds their customers. They already have watering holes, service providers, and software they use. Remember the three different spheres of influence we discussed at the beginning of this chapter. Some startups will use these insights to define who their customers are.

Is this a long way to say that there is no definitive answer? Kind of. Sunir Shah, CEO of AppBind, puts it like this: "Founders will do partnerships stuff before they invest in a partnerships team."[43] Your job as a founder is to know your customers really well. This includes anybody who influences them. You will also want to have a rough idea of which big companies could be potential acquirers of your business. All of these are potential partners. However, you should not lose sight of your main goal: to find product-market-fit. Once you are ready to scale, you can pour serious resources into partnerships.

WHAT DOES A PARTNER MANAGER DO ALL DAY?
Most partnership leaders fall into this career by accident. After all, there is no university class on partnerships. They often are founders, salespeople, or marketers at a seed stage company which found product-market-fit. Suddenly, their team is overwhelmed with requests from customers and somebody shouts: "Is anybody here a partnership expert?"

They then courageously step forward and give it a go. I often get messages from these people. Inevitably they will get lost and at some point straight up ask: "What does a partner manager do?"

Most people don't know. This hit me hard when I told a friend I was speaking at Catalyst, the leading conference of partnership professionals. He looked at me and said: "A partnership conference? What do you talk about? Recommendations for the best steakhouses in each city?"

Haha. I get it. All partnership people do is hang out with each other. Very original. But if you ask CEOs, I bet you they also think that's what we do. Grab dinner with partners. Gossip about the industry. Post on LinkedIn about the great meetings they had. Some partnership people are like this. But they don't tend to last very long.

So, what is our job? You might think it is to form partnerships. This is wrong. Your job is to help the company achieve its goals. Partnerships are one of many ways to get there. So at the highest level, partnership managers need to educate the company. When and how can partners help? When is it better not to partner?

At a high level, we do this through the company's build, buy, partner strategy. Your job at this stage is to gather information on which problems partners could help with. Then you need to identify if there are any partners that fit your criteria.

The main challenge here is to overcome your team's inherent bias to do everything in-house. As I said before, partnerships are not a department but a strategy for each department. You need to paint the vision for how partners help each team achieve their goals. As Jill Rowley, the former chief growth officer of Marketo, says: "You need to infuse partnerships into the DNA of your organization."[44]

Once you have sold your own team on a partnership, you will have to sell potential partners on the same idea. In that sense, partnerships aren't too different from venture capital. You raise resources, review a bunch of potential partners, say no to most of them, and then invest in the most promising ones. The main difference is that we often don't allocate cash but *social capital*. It's the potential to obtain resources, favors, or information through personal relationships.[45]

Partnerships require a lot of trust. They are risky, so the other side needs to believe that this time will be different. Or that you will at least do what you promised. This is where the steak dinners come in. Kind of. Jay LeBoeuf framed it like this: "Relationships are not with companies, but with people." Trust is also not built with companies, but with people. This is why partner managers spend a lot of time with steak-holders (get it?) at both their own and partner companies. They need to get to know them. Understand what their personal and company goals are. Establish lines of communication. Raise *social capital* for future partnerships.

I once was handed an existing partnership opportunity after a team member left. During our first meeting, my counterpart asked a simple question: "Why do we always seem to get stuck?"

I was somewhat aware of previous attempts to partner that were blocked by our product team. These false starts left a bitter taste with the partner. We ran out of *social capital*. Worse, we incurred *relationship debt*. The partner was reluctant to work with us based on our track record. There are other types of debt that founders have to deal with, like technical debt or student loans. But unlike those, relationship debt can't be paid off with hard work. It takes two to tango. This is why partnership people will defend their relationships and try to avoid debt at all costs.

This is important because there is a way to build trust and raise *social capital* at scale. On his podcast, Reid Hoffman, co-founder of LinkedIn, discussed how to build trust fast with Spotify's founder, Daniel Ek.[46] They described a simple formula for trust:

Trust = Consistency over Time

We trust our colleague of five years because we know them. We've worked with them for a long time. We know their performance is consistent. But as we discussed before, time kills deals. As a startup, you don't have time. Opportunities will close and you'll run out of money. The way to build trust fast is to have a reputation of trustworthiness. Don't write checks you can't cash. Be upfront about whether now is the right time to partner. If you commit, give it everything you've got. Then let your partners tell the world all about it. Their references and warm intros are a shortcut to *social capital*.

Another important task of a partner manager is to champion your partners within your own company. When we worked on an alliance deal with LinkedIn, my counterpart Michael Nussbaum sent me the following message: "You should look at me as the internal LinkedIn sponsor for Hopin. Educate me → I educate LinkedIn. Convince me → I convince LinkedIn."

There is no way you get to pitch all relevant stakeholders at your partner company yourself. You need a sponsor, somebody who holds up the flag when you aren't in the room. Once you have convinced your champion, you need to arm them. Give them whatever is necessary to sell internally on your behalf. You, of course, need to champion your partner inside your company as well. This insight and Mike's excellent stewardship allowed us to get the leadership of both companies aligned. A few months later, CNBC announced LinkedIn's investment of up to $50 million into Hopin as part of a wider partnership.[47]

Unlike VCs, partner managers can't lean back once they have invested. The occasional "How can I be helpful?" message won't do. This is where most partnerships go wrong. The partner manager signs a deal and immediately gets *shiny partner syndrome*: a new, more exciting opportunity comes along. They want to spend all their time there. But you can't open a door and then expect your team to walk through it. Only in Hollywood does the movie end when you kiss the bride. As any married couple knows, once the paper is signed the real work begins. You have to take your team by the hand.

Partnerships need to be launched and landed. Too often I hear partner managers complain that they are blocked by marketing. That their sales teams don't engage with partners. That product doesn't want to build the integration they asked for. There's a reason many successful partnership leaders are former entrepreneurs. They are not afraid to get their hands dirty. They do anything to win!

The wrong approach to enablement is to write a playbook nobody reads and host a workshop everybody forgets. The right approach is to lead by example. To do the job and show the results. To help your team win and let them take the credit. They need to feel the value first-hand. Only then will your team engage with partners.

Yes, you develop the strategy, but you also have to show each team why and how to work with partners. At your own company and at the partner company. Talk to every customer success manager at the partner company. Track all customer introductions in a spreadsheet if you have to. Craft your enablement material and host workshops. Join sales calls and pitch on behalf of the partner. Update both leadership teams. Force accountability through regular check-ins. Celebrate your wins so more people want to be a part of them. Hope is not a strategy. You make your own success.

This wide range of tasks explains why partnership leaders tend to be more senior in their organization. Fredrik Mellander, former head of partnerships at HR startup Teamtailor, shared that "A partnership is in many ways like running a company within a company."[48] You need to speak the language of each team you work with. Most partner managers are fluent in product management, sales, finance, customer success, strategy, and some even in software development. They understand every function of the business enough to show how the partnership will benefit them.

Okay, like, woah. That sounds like a lot of work. And it is.[49] Some roles like customer support are reactive. You work when people reach out to you. Partnerships are the opposite of that. You have to be proactive all the time. This is a real challenge for a lot of partner managers. They try to spin dozens of plates at the same time which is unsustainable.

Instead, similar to how a VC manages their startup portfolio, you have to learn how to manage your partner portfolio.

PARTNER PORTFOLIO MANAGEMENT

New partner managers all learn within a few months that they can't work on every opportunity. You have to pick a few partnerships and do them well. However, over time you will add on more and more partners. Your workload will creep up on you until you realize it is 11 p.m., you are on your sixth coffee, and you haven't showered today. To avoid this fate, partner managers need to develop the muscle to re-prioritize partners on a regular basis. I call this process *partner portfolio management*. Similar to a VC, you need to decide which opportunities you want to allocate your time and resources to. So, how do you know where to invest?

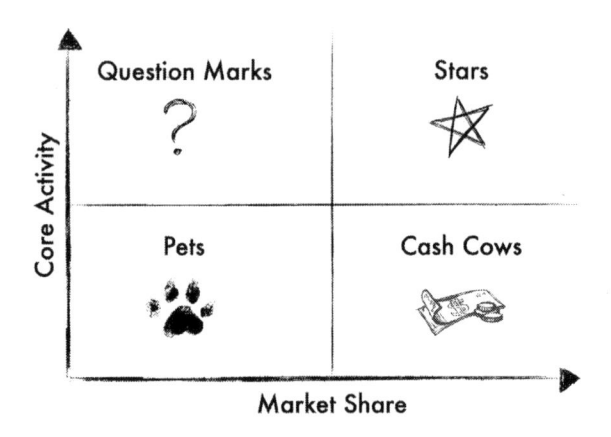

Fig. 7: Partner Prioritization Matrix.
Source: Altered version of BCG's Growth-Share-Matrix.

One of my favorite tools is the Partner Prioritization Matrix. It is based on Boston Consulting Group's "Growth-Share-Matrix."[50] This framework was designed to help companies decide which products, projects, and business lines deserve more resources. I have also found it to work well to help you decide where to spend your time and create a well-balanced partner portfolio. I always show this slide in strategy meetings and split our partners into four buckets:

Question Marks: These are high-growth opportunities, but your company hasn't been able to capture significant value from these partners yet. The goal here is to quickly validate if this is a good partner to work with. Do they really grow as fast as they say? Do they really have that many customers? Do their customers want to work with us? If the answer to these questions is yes, the partner becomes a "Star." If it is no, we discard them as "Pets."

Stars: This type of partner is the perfect mix of fast growth and your ability to capture all the value that comes with it. These partners have lots of future potential so you should pour your time, energy, and resources into them. Once growth stalls, they become "Cash Cows."

Cash Cows: These partners have a lot of shared customers, but they don't grow a lot. This often happens if you partner with very large companies like Salesforce for a long time. They have a loyal customer base and make more money from their existing customers than new ones. So, at some point your partnership will hit a ceiling. Most of your customers already work with the partner so there isn't a lot of room to grow. Your job here is to milk these "Cash Cows" and reinvest the profits into "Stars" and "Question Marks."

Pets: Slow growth and/or customer churn will sooner or later turn most "Question Marks" and "Cash Cows" into "Pets." They're called this because these partners are often kept around as pet projects. There is no current or future potential, so you should divest or reposition.

Why does prioritization matter? Because your job is to grow every quarter. Junior people often waste a lot of time on question marks and pets because they don't know better. Experienced partner leaders often invest in cash cows and forget to plant seeds. They don't develop the business further and are caught with their pants down once the milk runs out. This is why consistency is key. You need a process to validate, invest, milk, and discard opportunities in your portfolio.

If you struggle to find time to work on your most important partnerships, your first instinct should be to cut out some partners from your portfolio. That's because partnerships follow an extreme version of the 80/20 rule, where a small fraction of partners generate outsized returns for your business. We'll discuss this phenomenon in more detail in Chapter 4: Product Partnerships.

You don't always have to send them a breakup text though. It is often enough to move these partners into a self-serve workstream where you won't spend time with them unless their performance improves. If you still struggle to find time, the next step is to delegate.

The big mistake here is to point at a team member and say: "You are in charge now." Spoiler alert, they have other things to do. They often also won't know where to start. So, as I mentioned before, you will need to show your team how it is done first. This works especially well on sales calls.

At Hopin, our virtual events customers needed some way to get attendees to engage with event sponsors. This was important because without sponsors the organizers wouldn't have the money to pay for our platform. So I joined a sales call and pitched a partner tool which allowed you to gamify your events with a leaderboard. Attendees would win prizes if they visited sponsors and completed challenges. The organizers and sponsors would get amazing analytics and insights about their attendees. The customer loved it. Our salesperson took note. From then on, they used the exact same pitch on every customer with this problem. The best enablement is to show them how it's done.

Every partner's success story will lead to more successes. Your job as a partner manager is not to sit inside the flywheel and enjoy the ride. It's to stand on the outside and to push wherever help is needed. Build momentum and let others have fun. At some point, other team members will want to spin the wheel for you. Often, salespeople from both companies will connect with each other and start to strategize on their own.

Support people might create a group chat between the two companies to troubleshoot issues. This is great!

A big mistake partner managers make at this stage is to assume they need to be involved everywhere. You might think that your job is to talk to partners. That means you will feel threatened when somebody else talks to them. Don't. Your job is to infuse a partnership mindset into every department. Don't become the bottleneck for your company's growth. You have bigger fish to fry.

Yet at the same time never think you can be hands off. Without active orchestration from a partner manager, any partnership will grow stale and die. After a while the day-to-day issues take over. People become order takers. They put out fires all day. A new feature launch pulls them into a different direction. As the architect of the partnership, you need to sell the vision of the partnership and build on the momentum.

There is a flaw in this approach though. Yes, you can prioritize partners and delegate some of the execution. But this means that you will always have to make a decision about who to partner with. What if your decision is wrong, and a great partner decides to work with a competitor instead? On top of that, if you delegate, you still need to involve people. So your partnership efforts will always be bottlenecked by how many people you have who can work with these partners. The solution is to build a scalable program where people can decide to partner with you without your active involvement. We will discuss what this looks like later in the book.

Now that we have gone through the basics of partnerships, the rest of the book will cover each of the five types of partnerships in more detail so you can learn how to leverage them for your business.

CHAPTER 2:
MARKETING PARTNERSHIPS

"Fire bullets, then cannonballs."
—Jim Collins

DON'T BOIL THE OCEAN.
SHOOT FISH IN A BARREL.

When we founded our first startup, I shared my hiring woes with our mentor, Tim Davey, former co-founder of onefinestay. He gave me the following advice: "Hiring is always a slog. The only way to hack it is to have your own pool of pre-filtered candidates. That's why accelerators like Y Combinator work. They have a job board to which candidates apply and pre-filtered talent shifts between the different startups wherever it is needed."

What does this have to do with marketing partnerships? Turns out, a lot. When you hire for a role, you have to attract talent. When you market your product, you have to attract customers. In marketing, you hire for the role of customer. This means you have to get specific about what your ideal customer profile looks like. The same way you have to get specific about the type of person you want to hire.

At our startup, we cast our net into the open sea. We posted job ads on LinkedIn, Indeed, and any other place we could think of. We were over the moon when we received 100+ applications for each role. But the quality of those applicants was awful.

To give you an idea, we wanted to hire a marketer. One of the applicants had experience in "traffic management." On a closer look, I realized he did not mean web traffic. Traffic, traffic. He directed cars at street crossings.

Tim's advice acknowledged a simple truth. Both potential candidates and customers are strangers. You don't know them. You can't trust them. So you will have to filter through piles of irrelevant leads. The secret to recruitment and marketing partnerships is to find pools of customers that have already been vetted by a partner.

Y Combinator (YC) is a startup accelerator with a reputation for excellence. Previous portfolio companies include giants like Airbnb, Stripe, and Reddit. They are known for their rigorous interview process for founders. As we discussed before, trust is a function of consistency over time. YC has done a good job interviewing founders in the past, so you trust they will continue to do so. This means you can assume any startup which makes it into the program is somewhat better than average.

This creates a competitive advantage in hiring. The best job applicants will want to work at YC startups because they were pre-filtered by YC. There are a lot of scams and bad companies out there, so they trust that YC companies are better. On the flip side, if a YC founder interviews and hires a person, you can assume they also are above average. This allows you to skip some, but not all, steps when you want to hire them. In essence, YC is a lighthouse. A center of trust that attracts and connects excellent people with each other.

When trust is high, the speed of decisions goes up, and costs go down. YC startups can hire faster, which gives them an edge. The same is true for customers. You can cast your net into the open ocean. Spray and pray. But both you and your potential buyers are strangers to each other. You will both have to spend time to build trust, which slows things down.

The marketing partnership approach is to tap into communities, blogs, and other companies that have a pool of customers that trust them. Jay McBain calls these your customer's "watering holes." These partners filtered through the ocean already. Their customers believe them when they make a recommendation. Now all you have to do is shoot fish in a barrel. Easy.

Or so you think. Your partners have built their reputation with their audience and customers for years. The last thing they want is somebody to rush in with a megaphone and disrupt the conversations happening at the watering hole. Instead, great marketing partnerships acknowledge that you don't market through your partner. You market and evangelize together with the partner. You provide value to existing conversations. In the following chapter, we'll discuss what this looks like in practice.

THE FOUR FLAVOURS OF MARKETING PARTNERSHIPS

These types of marketing partnerships are what most people think of when they talk about partnerships. What's great is that they are also a foundational building block of all other partnerships. It's relatively easy to co-market with a partner compared to other types like product integrations, which take months. This makes them the ideal minimum viable partnership, a way to dip your toe in the water before you decide to cannonball. There are a few different types of co-marketing arrangements:

Affiliates: These are third parties that have some sort of special access to an audience. They might own a newsletter, a YouTube channel, or a blog. Their job is to promote your product in exchange for a finder's fee whenever somebody buys it. Most of the time they do this through a special link to your website or a discount code they share with their audience.

Referral partners: These are often confused with affiliate partners, but there is one key difference: the level of customer trust. While affiliates promote you to a broad audience, referral partners rely on a trusted network and personal connections to make introductions. For example, if a friend sends you an invite to sign up for a new American Express credit card, that's a referral.

There is an issue though. If your friend gets a commission for each new person who signs up for a credit card, their incentive might be different from yours. You want the best credit card; they want the money. As we mentioned before, misaligned incentives are one of the top reasons partnerships fail. So to maintain this trust, there needs to be something in it for the end-customer, too. That's why most credit cards offer both the referrer and referee a bonus when they sign up.

Influencers: We have all seen our favorite YouTube or Instagram creator give a shout out to a brand in one of their videos. These creators and thought leaders have built a lot of trust and *social capital* with their audience. So if they tell them to check out your website, many of them will. Again, the key difference between a partnership with a creator and a sponsorship or ad is trust.

At StreamYard, we only partner with creators who use our product to produce their live streams and video podcasts. This way we make sure that the endorsements are genuine and resonate with the creator's audience. Many influencers have shifted to this approach as well. Too often have creators "sold out" and promoted products they don't use themselves. That's why sponsorships have a bad rep. Because if money is the main motivator, it doesn't matter if you or your competitor sponsor a creator. They will promote both products equally.

This builds *relationship debt* with an influencer's audience. They trust the creator to recommend the best tool they use themselves, not random tools that pay them the most money. Even if the product isn't bad, if the wrong audience buys it, they will still have a poor experience.

Brand partnerships: The fluffiest of partnerships. The goal here is to associate yourself with another brand and generate as much buzz as possible. Press releases, viral social media posts, media features, you name it. Like when Snoop Dogg partnered with Martha Stewart. Brand partnerships are notorious in the partnerships world because they are hard to do well. It's hard to measure their impact and most of them will end as a flash in the pan. However, when done well they can be game-changing.

In January 2023, things didn't look too rosy for the launch of Greta Gerwig's latest movie, *Barbie*. It ranked forty-fifth in terms of interest among all the films tracked by the research site The Quorum. Much lower than *John Wick*, *Spider-Man*, and *Aquaman*, which were much more anticipated. Even before its launch, people had written the movie off as another aging franchise and money grab. No amount of Facebook ads or billboards could have turned this situation around. But *Barbie* had a secret weapon up her sleeves: partnerships.

In the lead up to *Barbie's* premiere, our social media feeds all turned pink. *Barbie* was everywhere. Want to stay in Barbie's Malibu dream house? Partnership with Airbnb. Want to travel like *Barbie*? Pink suitcases by Béis. Want to get your little boy excited about *Barbie*? Partnership with Hotwheels.

More than 100 brand partnerships went viral over the course of a few weeks. In an interview with Variety, Warner Bros. President of Global Marketing Josh Goldstine was asked about his marketing budget: "The reason people think we spent so much is that it's so ubiquitous. That's a combination of paid media and how many partners came to play with us."[51]

His team understood that the *Barbie* had the right mix of nostalgia and mass appeal. There were endless opportunities to generate what Josh called "earned media." Free publicity, courtesy of his partners.

At some point the hype took on a life of its own. Everybody wanted to partner with *Barbie*. This allowed his team to borrow credibility from other brands and reach entirely new audiences, like gamers through a *Barbie*-themed Xbox. Moreover, it activated super fans who decked themselves in with all things *Barbie*. These fans showed up in droves at the opening weekend, all dressed in pink. *Barbie* generated $1.4 billion at the box office and was the most successful global release in Warner Bros. history. Not bad for a mediocre movie.

Unless you are the next Facebook, your startup doesn't have the same mass appeal as Barbie. So, don't go out and try to partner with every possible company on the planet. Instead, focus on your customers. Identify the influencers, companies, and communities they trust. Then surround them.

MAKE YOUR PARTNER MARKETING POP

"I thought Hopin is a cool company so we should do something together." I got this message from a partner we integrated with. Needless to say, we did not "do something together." This is not how you approach co-marketing with partners. Another example of the cargo cult of partnerships that I mentioned before. He probably woke up that day, saw a competitor make an announcement, and wondered "Who could I do that with?" Leaf headphones! Here are two major issues with this pitch:

Christine Li, VP of partnerships at G2, shared that most partner managers pitch activities from the lens of their own business rather than the partners. I appreciate that you think we're "a cool company," but what is in it for me? Why would I want to go-to-market with you? More importantly though, what is in it for our customers?[52]

This brings us to the second issue. What does "do something together" even mean? This statement shows a clear lack of preparation. We all have a lot going on. Don't shoot off vague messages like this to your partners. Instead, take the approach Isaac Morehouse, CMO of Reveal, advocates for: figure out which customers you want to target. Then which partner can help you reach them. And finally, the activities you can do together.[53]

When you start with the customer, you also avoid *shiny partner syndrome*. Often a partner will have millions of people visiting their website every month. They dangle this traffic in front of you like a carrot. But how many of these people will actually use your product? This is the difference between the *Total Addressable Market (TAM)* and *Serviceable Obtainable Market (SOM)* of a partner. Identify your ideal customer profile, then segment your partner's audience. Focus only on the subset of your partner's audience that overlaps with the type of customers you want to reach. When you then compare potential partners, you might realize that a smaller, more focused partner could be a better fit.

One additional benefit of segmentation is that it makes it easier for you to figure out the "do something together" part. If you go in blind, everybody will stick to the same old marketing partnership activities: blog posts, press releases, social media posts. Yawn. Look at *Barbie's* case. They didn't ask Airbnb and Hotwheels to post on social media "check out the *Barbie* movie." Instead, they created a real-life Barbie dream house in Malibu for adults with wanderlust. And a series of Barbie-themed toy cars to get little boys excited about the movie. Two different customer segments. Two different partners. Two different activities.

One of the best parts of the job is to get creative with your partners on what activities you can do together. To prepare for this brainstorming session, I like to create a list of assets we have and how many viewers they get per month. Like your website, product, blog, social media, and so on. This is important because it helps you and your partner understand how many views you might get with each activity. There's no faster way to kill a partnership than to launch a blog post nobody reads. Then you also add features which are unique to your company to this list. Like Airbnb's deep understanding of real estate or Hotwheels expertise in toy cars.

At this point, you probably have dozens of ideas for activities already. Great. But activity ideas are easy. I could come up with 20 generic ones off the top of my head. In fact, here they are:

1. Blogs
2. Press release
3. Industry publications
4. Landing pages
5. Whitepaper
6. Email blast
7. Newsletter feature
8. In-product pop up
9. Podcasts
10. Youtube videos
11. Social media posts
12. Onboarding email embed
13. Limited time offers
14. Influencer content about joint solution
15. Joint webinar
16. Feature on your company's login screen
17. Joint sponsorship of an industry event
18. Special holiday offer
19. Email drip sequence
20. Presence at an owned events

See? Easy, but boring. Get creative. The more specific to your companies and customers, the better.

It makes sense to cast a wide net at this stage. Explore all possible ideas with your target partner. Shay Howe, CMO of marketing automation platform ActiveCampaign, took this approach when he worked on an alliance with Salesforce. He created a slide deck with 50+ co-marketing ideas, including high-fidelity mockups and the expected reach of each activity. One idea was to walk Salesforce CEO Marc Benioff's dog while dressed as the ActiveCampaign logo. Needless to say, Salesforce declined.

Why would Shay invest so much time and effort into ideas that will never happen? Because he had a key insight: "No" is safe. "No" gives comfort. With every "No" you hear from a partner, you can ask questions and learn more. Inch by inch, you get a better understanding of what your partner cares about. Then you refine your ideas and try again.[54]

Most of the time you won't land on a Barbie Malibu dream house. As Shay shared: "It's tempting to think that there is THE thing that works magic. . . . The most successful campaigns are not just a GTM (go-to-market) campaign. It's, "How do we run the life cycle of this? How do we continue to grow together?"

Barbie's brand partnerships hyped up the movie premiere, but nobody talks about them anymore today. These types of PR partnerships aren't good enough for most startups. You don't need a flash in the pan. You need sustainable growth. This is what Shay means with "run the life cycle." The best way is to focus on processes, not one-off promotion. Figure out how your product is relevant to each other's customer journey and hit up the customer in just the right moment.

Take Oyster, an employer-of-record startup, for example. Oyster makes it easy for companies to employ people in a compliant way anywhere around the world. They invest a lot in partnerships with VC funds and accelerators. Why? Because if a startup just received money from a VC, they need to hire! But it's not enough to get a VC to post on social media about you. Instead, Oyster made sure to be a crucial part of the VCs onboarding process for startups.

They mastered the value exchange we outlined in the Partner Value Triangle. Oyster makes it easy for startups to employ people around the world. People abroad are often cheaper to hire, which is a win for startups. But it is also a win for VCs, because startups don't spend all of the money the VC gave them on San Francisco salaries. Cheaper hiring is a competitive advantage. Pair this with a compelling referral offer for the startup and VCs will make sure their entire portfolio signs up.

We took a similar approach at StreamYard. In 2020, LinkedIn was very restrictive about who could live stream on their platform. Live streams are difficult to moderate. One wrong stream could be a PR nightmare for a professional network like LinkedIn. Still, we decided to partner with them and share our expertise. Over the following two years, we worked with LinkedIn to improve the live experience and find ways to open it up to more users in a safe way.

To repay the favor, LinkedIn featured us as a preferred partner in their live stream onboarding flow. Every time somebody signs up to live stream on LinkedIn, they see our free trial offer. Through our partnership, we were able to reach customers at the point of sign up, far earlier than any competitor could. This wasn't a big deal back then, but today millions of people live stream on LinkedIn. Most of them use StreamYard.

Another key insight from these stories is that you need to own a specific niche with your partners and customers. When a VC or startup thinks about remote hiring? Oyster. When LinkedIn or a creator thinks about live streaming? StreamYard. Don't try to be everything to everybody. Oyster offers a whole range of features and so does StreamYard. But the more targeted the use case and pitch, the more likely it is to be remembered in the right moment.

This applies to all types of partnerships. Imagine you are, for example, the go-to service provider for German speaking customers. Every sales rep should immediately think of you as soon as somebody starts a call with "Guten Tag." You might speak English as well. You might even have English-speaking customers. But your competitive edge is being German. You better show up to every meeting in your Lederhosen and own that niche.

An important concept to consider is what I call the SaaS Buying River.[55] Consumers might buy a Barbie-themed Hot Wheels car before or after they watched the *Barbie* movie. But for customers of software-as-a-service (SaaS) startups, timing matters.

At Hopin, customers first bought their virtual events platform and then looked at what other partners they wanted to hire. Like a virtual photo booth for their audience to snap selfies. However, customers had already bought their virtual events platform before they ever talked to the photo booth company. The photo booth partner had no way to ever send us a new virtual events customer. Leads only flow downstream in the *SaaS Buying River*.

Delya Jansen, former director of alliances at Snowflake and NetApp, suggested a useful exercise in our podcast episode: jot down your customer's buying journey. In what order do they purchase all the tools they use to solve a specific problem? Then unfurl your customer's ecosystem. Instead of a circular shape that surrounds your customer, map it against this linear timeline. When do they look at each influencer, service partner, and tool you previously identified?[56]

This exercise makes sure you set the right goals for each marketing campaign. Tools that are downstream from you can be great marketing partners. You could, for example, advertise new features to expand your existing customer base. But if you want to find new customers, market with partners that are upstream from your product.

LEVEL UP YOUR MARKETING PARTNER PROGRAM
Unfortunately, it is not enough if your partner is hyped up about your marketing activities. Your team needs to agree to them, too. I am a big believer that partnership people shouldn't be afraid to roll up their sleeves and write a blog post or create graphics themselves. But the truth is that your marketing team is a key stakeholder in all these activities. If marketing partnerships are your main focus, it makes sense for the partnerships team to be part of the marketing department.

This move will help with goal alignment. Marketing teams are often afraid that any partner activity is another item on their plate. Something they do for you as a favor. A distraction from their actual work. This is wrong. The goal of a marketing partnership is to drive results. To help your marketing team achieve their key performance indicators (KPIs) and move the company forward.

Still, it might take some time for your marketing team to see the light. Partnerships can be fluffy. Your team has probably been burnt by a Barney partnership in the past. That's when they had to write a blog not for their customers to read, but to show a partner how much they love them. These activities don't drive results. Customers don't care if you love a partner. They want to know what's in it for them. You need to align the incentives of all parties of the partner value triangle.

Ryan Lieser, VP of partnerships & alliances at Anecdotes, shared the following playbook: First, figure out what your marketing team cares about. What are the strategic initiatives they want to promote this quarter? It is easier to figure out what marketing is interested in first than try to force a random idea down their throat. Instead, fit the right partner to their initiatives. Always quantify the expected reach for each activity. How many eyeballs will you get? Why do customers care? Marketing wants to see a return on investment (ROI) for any time they spend on partners.

Assumptions are not enough, though. You will need to prove the ROI if you want real buy-in. Since you don't have any actual data to go by, your first co-marketing experiment with a partner will require a leap of faith from your marketing team. Make it as easy as possible for them to say yes. Draft the social media copy. Accumulate statements from partners.

Ensure that your first activity is something small and lightweight to test the waters.

Once you have a few wins under your belt, your marketing team might become partner pilled. If this is the case, Ryan recommends you lock in those wins. Ask them to commit to cross-department KPIs focused on partner marketing. This way partners are top of mind whenever the marketing team reviews their goals for the quarter.

Another way to ensure buy-in is to hand over ownership. At the start, hold your own marketing team and your partner by the hand. Facilitate the collaboration where you can. But over time, hand over the project as well as future activities. Assign a dedicated contact on your marketing team and the marketing team of your partner. People love to take responsibility for exciting projects. It is also fun to work with partners and a great learning experience. You get to peek into another company and see how they operate. The right, ambitious person on your team will leap on this opportunity.

You know you have reached this stage when team members on both sides start to collaborate without your involvement. Just remember that you can never go fully hands-off. Without active orchestration by a partner pro, any partnership will grow stale and die. You still need to inject energy and new ideas on how to grow the partnership on a regular basis.

If your own marketing team is bought in, you are only halfway there. You also need to convince your partner's marketing team. This task is too important to leave it up to your counterpart. Instead, make it as easy as possible for them to do their job.

It starts with what we call a *memorandum of understanding* (MOU). This is a document which outlines everything you and your partner have discussed. Often this is a multi-page doc, but I have found that nobody reads those. Instead, I prefer one simple slide with three columns: committed partner activities, support and resources required, and any contractual terms like revenue share if applicable. This is a great asset to send to anybody who wants to get up to speed on what this partnership is about.

You might also add another slide with context about your company in case the marketing team never heard of you. But that's it. Two slides. Marketing people spend a lot of time on TikTok, so you can't expect them to read more. Bonus points of your MOU is a TikTok video.

But don't actually post it on TikTok. The MOU will contain lots of private information. I bet your competitors would love to know how many users you have or the open rate of your email newsletter. This is why many companies will ask you to sign a nondisclosure agreement (NDA) before they share this information.

An NDA can be a useful way to build trust. Just know that no matter what, always make sure this document is mutual. If a partner wants you to keep their info confidential but reserves the right to snitch on you, that's a bad sign. NDAs should also help speed up the process, not slow it down. I have seen lawyers who negotiated an NDA for weeks. This seems pointless. Far less than 1% of NDAs ever get litigated. So, why waste time on them?

Instead, take a look at OneNDA.org. It's a free NDA template created by some of the top lawyers in the world. They were fed up with the endless negotiations on what should be a standard document. So they created the gold standard. It is the same agreement that Coca-Cola, Panasonic, and thousands of other companies use. The best part is that you can't change it. Some large companies will still want to use their own NDA, but most other partners will sign a OneNDA on the spot. It's a win-win.

On the other hand, there is no short-cut for your partner agreement. You might get away without an agreement for light co-marketing activities. But the more involved the partnership becomes, the higher the stakes. When the stakes are high, you need solid paper. I used to downplay contracts as bureaucracy, and I still think this is true. If you need to call up your partner, point at a contract, and say "See, you promised to do X," then the partnership is already beyond repair. Most disagreements can be fixed through transparent communication.

But agreements become really important when things turn south. Think about the opening story of this book. A partner pulled a bait-and-switch on our customers. They were what we call in partnerships, *assholes*. Sooner or later, you will encounter one of them as well. In those moments, you need to have a clear understanding on how to terminate the relationship. How soon can we terminate? What will happen to joint customers or intellectual property? And who will pay for any damages? Expect the best, but always prepare for the worst.

CHAPTER 3:
SERVICE & CHANNEL PARTNERS

"Show me the incentive and
I'll show you the outcome."
—Charlie Munger

WHY DO STARTUPS NEED SERVICE & CHANNEL PARTNERS?

In this chapter, we will discuss how you can attract service and channel partners to work with your business. This is quite the extensive topic, so the goal is not to give you a detailed guide. Instead, I will give you some rough ideas on what to look out for and additional resources if you want to dig in further. You probably also noticed that service and channel partners were two separate rungs in the partnership's pyramid. Are they the same?

Not every service partner, also known as *systems integrator (SI)*, will want to sell your product. They will often be more than happy for you to do all the sales so they can focus on what they do best. Services. Likewise, not all channel partners will provide services after they sell your product. But traditional channel sales are on the decline.

Channel partners are companies that work with manufacturers or producers to sell their products on their behalf. In the past, if you wanted to sell software you had to go to a reseller like RadioShack and convince them to put your CDs on their shelves. The internet has disrupted this business model.

Today, you can buy most products directly online. Why would anybody want to pay a premium to buy from a reseller? The only rational explanation is if the reseller would also offer something else on top. They could bundle their own software together with yours, so customers don't have to manage two different contracts and invoices. Or they sell their own services together with your product.

We call these partners *value-added resellers* (VARs). They tend to receive the same training as service partners, like certifications. On top of that, you also teach them how to sell your software. Because of these similarities, we will discuss them in the same chapter.

So, why would a startup want to work with channel and service partners? Because every software startup faces the same issue: Customers don't like to pay for software. That's because they know that once a piece of software is written, it costs the company almost nothing to add another user. So, why charge so much?

These customers, of course, overlook the fact that building a software product is expensive. Not just the engineers and their big Silicon Valley salaries, but also the starting up costs, infrastructure expenses, and risks you need to be repaid for. That's why startups tend to charge based on the value they provide to customers, not the cost of the materials they use to create their product. Or, in the words of their customers: that's why startups charge too much.

There is one thing, however, that customers love to pay for: services. There's something visceral about them. You talk to a person. You see the hours they put into your project. Then you review the results together. Of course, you would want this person to be compensated fairly. Even if it is irrational.

Like when you feel forced to tip 30% at a restaurant because the waiter told you their life story. But here's the catch: startups love software and avoid services.

Services are a low-margin, high-maintenance business. At Hopin, we could charge $10,000 and more to have a dedicated person on call during an event. It sounded like a great deal because the hourly wage of that person was not $10,000. They wished it was $10,000. However, that person needed to be hired, trained, and available during that time. They were also on our payroll even if no customer needed their service, which created fixed costs for our business.

Worst of all, services don't scale well with demand. A service heavy business is quicker to experience bottlenecks. During the pandemic, one of our main competitors in virtual events offered a 3D, metaverse type experience. It required a lot of manual work from their team to create a virtual world for each customer. Our experience was more like a Zoom call.

In April 2020, at the height of the pandemic, I was on a call with a customer who lectured me on how the metaverse is the future. He also felt the need to tell me that he will go with this competitor instead. This was at 10 a.m. By 4 p.m., he sent me another message: "Your competitor said that their order books are full until November. Can we sign a $45,000 contract today?"

The mistake this competitor made was to rely too much on in-house services. A quick fix for the fact that their software was too complicated. Customers couldn't set it up themselves, so the competitor sold the event creation as a service. When the pandemic struck and customers banged down their doors, they could not hire fast enough to meet the demand. They lost the opportunity to make hundreds of millions. Companies who partnered or built simpler software had the advantage.

The same applies to sales. If your product is complicated, customers will want to call with your sales team to see if it meets their requirements. Even if your product is simple but expensive, customers will still want to talk to a human. Again, there is something visceral here. If people have to pay you tens or hundreds of thousands of dollars for your product, they feel like they deserve a call. Just for their own comfort and so they can tell their boss that they did their due diligence. But a sales team is expensive.

At its peak, Hopin had more than 400 customer-facing employees. Sales, customer success, event services, you name it. This, in hindsight, was a grave mistake. Events are a seasonal business, so during the quieter months we paid through the nose for all those people. During peak months, we needed extra help. And when the demand for virtual events declined after the pandemic, we had several rounds of layoffs. All this is bad for employee morale and your business as a whole.

That's the reason why VC investors don't like service-heavy businesses. As a startup, the gold standard is to achieve a 10 times revenue multiple at your initial public offering

(IPO). This means that if your company has $100 million in annual recurring revenue, it will ideally be valued at $1 billion. Unicorn status.

Investors will want to look under the hood of your business though. The same way you might check the engine of a car before you buy it. What they expect to find under the hood is a well-oiled, software-based growth engine. Because once the software is written, it costs very little to onboard a new customer. Software businesses get to keep most of the money they make, or in business speak, they have great profit margins.

Investors don't want to discover that you in reality are a Fred-Flintstone car. Something that looks like a software startup but is actually powered by 400 people pedaling as fast as they can. If that's the case, investors will discount your company hard. Manual labor doesn't scale. It is also too risky that your team might stop pedaling and relax in Bali once you cashed in on those IPO shares.

There are two ways startups can bridge this gap: simplify your business or build a partner program. The first option is a great idea for any startup. You should always try to keep your business lean and focused. If your product is so easy to use that customers don't need help, that's great! This isn't always possible though. Often the customer will want something complex, and that requires a more robust product.

A partner program allows you to recruit experts, consultants, agencies, and other companies that want to provide services around your business. The idea is that you offload a lot of manual labor to them so you can focus on your product instead. Partners will take on the burden of hiring, training, managing, and firing people for you. This makes sense if those activities aren't core to your business. If you're in doubt, look up your *build, buy, partner strategy* again.

As I mentioned before, customers love to pay for services. This is why there will never be a shortage of people who will want to offer services around your business. It can be very profitable. There are 132,000+ credentialed Salesforce experts around the globe.[57] These partners lead 70% of all Salesforce implementations. In 2023, Salesforce itself had close to 80,000 employees. The company's ecosystem created far more jobs than the company itself. And these are just their service partners.

Even better, Salesforce partners make $6.91 for every $1 of software that Salesforce sells. This is how profitable it is to sell services and tools on top of another platform. You might wonder why Salesforce would be okay to leave so much money on the table. Surely, they don't need to give partners that much?

The 7:1 ratio shows how much value you need to share with your partners to make it worth their time. Every dollar Salesforce makes comes from software, which has high margins. They get to keep most of that dollar. A lot of the seven dollars partners make comes from services. These are low-margin. A lot of the money is used for salaries instead of a fancy Salesforce tower in San Francisco.

Salesforce is happy with this deal because partners take on a lot of the fixed costs and heavy lifting that comes with services. If the economy booms, partners are the ones who will need to rush to double their headcount. All Salesforce needs to do is lean back and count their money. At the same time, if the economy turns south and Salesforce has a bad year, their partners will need to lay off people first. This saves the company a lot of hassle and bad press. Partners take on all the risk that comes with hiring and managing people, so it is only fair that they are rewarded for it.

ARE YOU THE RIGHT FIT FOR YOUR PARTNERS?

Service and channel partners aren't for everybody. There are some downsides to this approach. One is that you have less ownership of the customer relationship. This can make sense for companies which have found product-market-fit. But if you are still in search-mode, you need direct customer feedback. Every sales call or escalation to customer support can have valuable insights that you need to iterate on your product. Secondhand information from partners just won't cut it.

Another reason why you should wait until you have product-market-fit. Partners don't like to work with unproven startups. The whole idea of a partnership is to share both risks and profits. For early-stage startups, the risks are high and the profits unpredictable. This makes it hard to convince an agency or consultant to invest time and effort into learning your product. They don't have the luxury of deep pocketed investors. Partners need profits right now. Your sales team might be happy for you to change your sales pitch every week. But if you do this to a partner, they will drop you instantly. They need to know that your go-to-market approach works.

In his book, *Building Successful Partner Channels,* Hans Peter Bech also writes that channel partners will only want to work with startups that can become the market leader.[58] That's because software is a winner-takes-all business: the market leader will have exponentially more customers than the second most popular startup. Every customer will want to use the best product and software doesn't have a limit on how many users it can support. Customers crowd around the top. Partners want to be where the customers are.

We saw this at Hopin firsthand. We were the market leader in virtual events. At our peak we received over 1,000 inbound leads per day. Partners flocked to us in droves, and we enlisted hundreds of them to help sell and service our product. But most of our competitors had to sign up agencies one at a time and could never maintain partnerships with more than 10 agencies. They simply didn't have enough customers to make it worth the partner's time.

Hans Peter Bech also points out that not every go-to-market strategy and service requirements are the right fit for partners. There are two factors that matter to your sales team and channel partners: How much money will a customer spend (*deal size*), and how long does it take to close a deal (*sales cycle*)? These two factors are directly correlated.

Larger deals take longer to close. The graphic below shows how the interest of service and channel partners changes depending on the length of your sales cycle.

Fig. 8: Channel Partner Interest Graph.
Source: Franz-Josef Schrepf, inspired by Hans Peter Bech.

Let's say your goal is to make $10 million this year and you sell $1,000 software. You will have to onboard 10,000 customers to reach your goal. That's a lot of customers. You won't be able to spend much time with them. You can't even have a call with all of them. You'd have to do 30 calls per day. Every day. Including weekends. And that assumes every single call leads to a sale. The only way to achieve this goal is to be low-touch. Have customers sign up via your website. No call needed. Make the product so simple that they don't need your help to use it.

But wait, if customers don't need to call sales and the product is super simple, what can partners offer them? Nothing. Nada. Zilch.

Low-touch, low-deal size, high-volume products are not a great fit for partners. There isn't enough money to be made per customer. There may be small services a consultant can pick up. An agency might mention your software to a client in exchange for a small referral fee. But in most cases, there is not enough money changing hands to support a fully-fledged partner program.

On the flip side, you might sell real big deals to enterprises. If your product costs $10 million, then you need to close only one customer per year. Your sales cycle can be 12 months or even longer. But this still won't be attractive to partners. If you only have one customer per year, you can pass them to only one partner per year. All other partners leave empty-handed. Only giant, *global systems integrators* like Accenture would be willing to take on this type of risk.

The sweet spot for channel and service partners is in the middle. A price high enough to show that there is money to be made with services but low enough that a deal can be closed in less than 12 months. If your product fits these criteria, there will be a lot of agencies and consultants who will be interested. They can add you to the portfolio of products that they offer to their customers at relatively low risk. It won't take long to learn your product and they'll know within less than 12 months whether it was worth their time.

You won't have to hand over all your customers to partners either. Even a partner-centric company like Salesforce often has a premium services team for their largest customers. That's because these customers are too important. They are core to your company's success. If you only have one customer who is worth $10 million and they leave, your company is dead. They are too valuable to let any third party handle the relationship with them. We call this *customer concentration risk*.

Salesforce lets their partners manage the majority of smaller customers instead. They are big enough to be valuable for partners, but small enough that no single customer could tank the company's revenue. The same goes for their partners. While it is okay to focus on some large partners, be mindful of how many customers each partner has access to. You could create *partner concentration risk*. If one partner controls all of your customer relationships, they have a lot of leverage to negotiate a better deal for themselves. This can create the *channel conflict,* an issue we will discuss later in this chapter.

HOW TO FIND YOUR PARTNERS IN ~~CRIME~~ BUSINESS
How do you know if your product is right for service and channel partners? Figure out if you already have some. I call this your *shadow partner program*. The best partner programs aren't built, they are uncovered. There is no need to call random agencies and ask if they would like to work with

you. It all starts with your customers. Listen to them: what problems do they have? Who do they hire to solve them?

Of course, this assumes that you already have customers who use your product. But as we discussed in chapter 1 of this book: "Customers first, partners second." If you don't already know who your customers are, channel partners can't help you. They have their own business to run. A channel partner will want to be sure that they will make money. I mean that your solution can help their customers. But you get the gist. Only then will they invest time in the training needed to service and sell your product.

Still, if you're not ready to ask your customers about the partners they use yet, there are other ways to figure out if your product could benefit from service partners. One easy way is to search on freelance marketplaces like Fiverr. Type in the name of your product and see if any gigs pop up. For Hopin, we found dozens of gigs like "I will produce your virtual event" with hundreds of reviews. We knew there was something there.

Another way to uncover your *shadow partner program* is to look into your customer accounts. Chris Samila, chief partner officer at Partnership Leaders, shared a great hack with me: If you are a software company, download a list of all your customer accounts and the users in each team. Then compare email addresses. Let's say your customer is Google. You'd expect all team members in their account to have *@google.com* email addresses. If you find a user with a different email, like *abc@agency.com*, they are probably an agency.

Those are the best partners. They already know how to use your product. And if they work with Google, there's a high chance they might have other large customers as well. Help them sell your product and additional services to those clients, too. Another example of how you can turn a service partner into a channel partner.

As I mentioned in chapter 1, you can also ask your own sales and customer success teams who you should partner with. They will often have informal relationships with customers who double as consultants or agencies. This is how we found our initial cohort of 10 channel partners at Hopin.

It also helps to pay close attention to who is interested in your startup. How can you use their attention? Bruno Guerra Cunha, first partnership hire at HR startup Oyster, noticed his company received tons of interest from VCs. Their ideal customers are startups, so he saw an opportunity. He convinced his CEO to only talk to VCs who also promoted their solution to their startup portfolio. Not only did Oyster raise over $200 million+ from VCs, it also converted their interest into a valuable channel.[59]

There is another great source of potential partners: your partner's partners. Tai Rattigan, former head of global partnerships at analytics startup Amplitude, used this strategy to expand into Korea and Japan.[60] These markets are notoriously hard to penetrate on your own. Language barriers and different business practices make it close to impossible to go direct. So the team at Amplitude decided to find a value-added reseller for each region. But how?

Big names like Fujitsu are the obvious choice. But they are huge conglomerates. What do they know about Amplitude's startup customers? Instead, Tai turned to his partners at Braze, a customer engagement platform. Amplitude and Braze's products were a match made in heaven. Their teams sold their solutions as a bundle to customers in the US and Europe on a daily basis. He knew that Braze already had a foothold in Korea, so he asked who they worked with.

His contact at Braze pointed him toward a small Korean startup. Their core business was not to resell software. They had their own products. But they often resold Braze and serviced it in Korean because it worked so well with their own tool. Amplitude was a perfect addition to this mix, so soon this startup sold all three products as a bundle in Korea. They also hosted user meetups and workshops. This small startup basically became Amplitude Korea. There is no way Tai could have found them if it wasn't for a partner introduction.

OVERCOME CHANNEL CONFLICT AND WIN TOGETHER

Once you have uncovered your initial partners, the next step is to align your incentives. As I mentioned in chapter 1, incentives are one of the main reasons a partnership fails. A partner is a third party that you introduce into the relationship you have with your customer. You also introduce their business model into the mix. How will the partner make money from this relationship?

You might think that the easiest way to incentivize partners to send you business is a referral fee. You make $20 thousand. Then drive up to your partner in your black convertible. You lower your sunglasses and say: "Here are $2Gs. Treat yourself." And drive off into the sunset. So cool. So easy.

The problem is that this is not how partnerships work. Remember, Salesforce partners make close to $7 for every $1 Salesforce makes. Your partner needs to hire a lot of people. They provide labor-intensive, low-margin services, while you sell easy to replicate, high-margin software. These partners have higher expenses than you, so they will want to make more money than you! A referral fee just won't cut it.

Your job is to help the partner find ways to sell services alongside your product. This will make them a lot more money! I only realized this after weeks of tracking agency referrals in spreadsheets. It's a messy, frustrating process. Our average deal was around $25,000, so we were doling out $2,500 checks. One day I asked an agency owner how much money she makes if we refer a customer to her. "About $50,000," she mentioned in passing. I dropped my coffee mug. And the referral fee right along with it. She didn't need our $2,500. The agency owner needed more customers.

The funny part is that if you ask an agency if they would like a referral fee, they will of course say yes. Because . . . why not? It's free money. But also, a huge pain to track. As our Chief Business Officer, Armando Mann, told me: "Don't disrupt the agency's own business model." Don't invent new revenue streams. Help them find more customers for their existing offering and business model.

There are some cases in which referral fees and revenue share agreements do make sense. One is to leverage them as a short-term bonus for the partner's sales team. This is known as a *sales performance incentive fund,* or SPIFF. A $2,000 referral fee won't make a difference for your channel partner. But what if you give it directly to the sales rep who closed the deal? Jackpot![61]

These types of initiatives can help you introduce your product to the partner sales team. They will be excited to mention your product to all their customers! The problem is that they will mention it for the wrong reasons. Sure, your product might solve a customer need. But all they really care about is the bonus.

This creates an awkward dynamic. Drop the bonus and they stop mentioning your product. Worse, the partner might threaten to switch to a competitor who offers a larger bonus. If your market is commoditized, this creates a race to the bottom. You erode your margin as you try to keep up with the ridiculous referral fees your desperate competitors offer. In this situation, the customer always loses. Because they want the best product. Not the one that pays the highest fees to the sales rep.

That's why this type of incentive should be temporary at best. To grease the wheel until the partnership flywheel starts to spin. An alternative version that often leads to longer term success is to create a *marketing development fund (MDF)* for each channel partner.

Instead of paying out referral fees to the company, you put them into a pot which is used to pay for co-marketing activities. The partner can decide where they want to spend it. Social media ads? Booths at a trade show? Video testimonials from your shared customers? MDFs perfectly align both partners around a common goal: to win more customers. This should always be your objective when you design incentives for your partners. Because if they are misaligned, you will create *channel conflict*.

Channel conflict happens when you and your partners compete for the same business. This is less of an issue with service partners. The incentives here are clear: Your company sells the product; your partner offers the services around it. You nicely separated out which part of a customer's budget you go after. But with channel partners, this can become a huge mess.

I experienced this firsthand during the early days of Hopin's agency program. One day, one of our salespeople complained to me that an agency she had introduced to a customer had stolen her deal. We gave the agency a discount on each license they sold. The agency owner realized they could pass this discount onto the customer. They would make less money, but this could bind the customer to them in the long run. That's right, the agency lost both of us money because they wanted to own this account. As Charlie Munger said: "Show me the incentive and I'll show you the outcome." The incentives were misaligned, so we stepped on each other's feet.

The antidote to channel conflict is clarity. The rules of engagement need to be clear to all parties involved: the partner, your shared customer, and your team. The reason why the agency stole a deal from our sales rep was because they saw a fault in the system. Once we called it out and adjusted our agreement, the issue went away. However, this might often turn into a game of whack-a-mole.

The issue with agencies and consultants is that they are heavily commoditized. As a customer, I often don't care if I go with one or another as long as they get the job done. This means channel partners need to either compete on price, which hurts their bottom line, or they need to find ways to edge out the competition. This often means they will game the system. While competition between channel partners is healthy, if they compete with you, it will hurt all parties involved. If you go out of business, so do your channel partners.

To escape this game once and for all, Nelson Wang recommends the creation of *partner swim lanes*.[62] The idea is to slice up your customer base and market to make it easy for everybody to understand when they are allowed to engage. Four potential types of swim lanes include geography, segmentation, vertical, and capabilities.

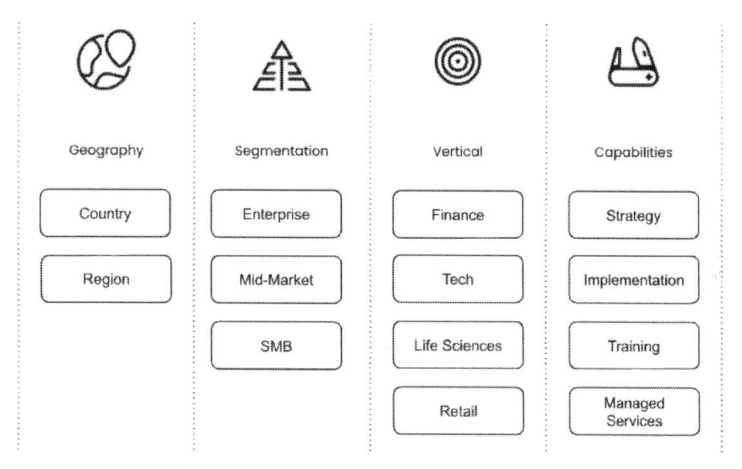

Geography	Segmentation	Vertical	Capabilities
Country	Enterprise	Finance	Strategy
Region	Mid-Market	Tech	Implementation
	SMB	Life Sciences	Training
		Retail	Managed Services

Fig. 9: Partner Swim Lanes. Source: Nelson Wang, partnerprinciples.com

If each party stays in their lane, there is no conflict. For example, at Hopin, we had a large group of customers in Germany. However, after an initial attempt to establish a German subsidiary, we realized that this market isn't core to our business. Our build, buy, partner decision shifted from build to partner. So any customer who needed German language sales or support would be redirected to a local partner.

Another way we sliced up our offering was based on customer needs. Each account still had its own Hopin customer success manager, but if they needed video production services, we always referred them to a partner. We didn't have the skills or setup for these requests. Salesforce segments their customers with their premium services team. Any customer above a certain size will be handled in-house. All others can be serviced by partners.

The criteria for these decisions needs to be easy to understand and communicated to all parties. Still, some channel conflict will be unavoidable. That's because you don't control the customer inbound. The customer decides who they talk to first, even if it's unintended. In those moments, Nelson recommends that the customer should be free to work with whomever they prefer. As long as the customer wins, everybody wins.

In those moments, however, measurement will become an issue at larger companies. Was this client partner-sourced? Or if we close an agency's deal, was it partner-influenced? Does marketing get the credit? Or sales? Should the partner get commission? It gets confusing really fast. There have been decades of debates around this topic, so I won't go into detail here. The way you measure the impact and success of your service and channel partners will be highly specific to the parties involved. The good news is that as a startup, you don't care. Money is money. All that matters is the deal closed. Don't let internal politics get in the way.

If you have a lot of partners, sooner or later you will run into a bad actor. Like the agency I mentioned in the preface of this book. You've waited long enough, so let me tell you how one of my first partnerships failed. Hard.

Our initial pilot program focused on 10 agencies around the globe. One of these partners saw our rocket ship rise and got jealous. It wasn't enough for them to charge for services. They wanted to charge for software, too. So they decided to build their own virtual events platform. This is not a problem in itself. If you think you can build a better tool, go ahead. It's the free market. Cut all ties and may the best product win.

Unfortunately, this is not what happened. We were lucky to find out early when a frustrated and confused customer contacted us. The agency deployed a bait-and-switch that went like this:

The partner exaggerated their position in our program. They told their clients that they were exclusive resellers of our software. All communication had to go through the partner. Customers were not allowed to contact Hopin's own customer support under penalty of death. Or at least that's what the customers made it sound like.

One day, a client asked for Hopin to complete a *Data Processing Agreement*. This is a standard request, but the agency saw an opportunity to stall. They claimed Hopin was unresponsive. As the event came closer, the client grew desperate. That's when the partner suggested the client should switch to the agency's own software. A low-quality copycat. The email they sent to the customer literally read: " . . . our own updated version of Hopin."

In hindsight, I should have known something was wrong. Two months earlier, one of their clients came to us with a similar issue. The client had hosted an event with that same agency, liked the platform, and now wanted to buy their own license. The agency claimed the customer had to buy through them. When our support team told the client that this was not the case, they were furious. The client canceled all future engagements with the partner.

The agency was furious, too. They lost a customer and said it was our fault. At the time, I didn't see the full picture. Likely due to sleep deprivation. The agency's CEO told me about all the other partnerships they had with tech companies. How they had much better structures and how well they worked. So I assumed it was my inexperience that led to the issue. Yet the partner always wanted more: Exclusive rights to work with certain customers. Preferential treatment. Discounts on our software. The list goes on.

Now I had email evidence that this partner was, in fact, what we in partnerships call an *asshole*. We were lucky to catch these bad actors before they could do any serious harm. That's why we decided against litigation. We still terminated the partnership, but lawsuits are a different game. They take time and energy away from the things that matter. Still, this partner represented our company in the market. Their bad behavior shattered trust with our customers.

Now the important question: Was this *channel conflict*? Channel conflict arises when there is a mismatch in incentives. The partner was clearly unhappy with our program and the benefits we offered them. They struggled with one of the fundamental issues of partnerships. A loss of control. They wanted to own the customer experience end to end. Something we could not offer them.

What makes this situation different is the reason the partner wanted control over the process. Customers did not value the services the partner provided. They wanted to work with us directly instead of paying for partner services they did not need. This issue did not occur with our other partners. The agency was bad at their job and tried to make up for it through shady business practices.

This is the difference between a genuine partner who experiences *channel conflict* and a bad actor. With channel conflict, all parties in the *partnership value triangle* engage to create value. However, the incentives might be misaligned and the rules unclear, so people step on each other's toes. As long as there is a shared foundation of trust, this issue can be fixed through clear swim lanes. If a partner is unhappy with your program, difficult to work with, or pushes for win-lose outcomes, disengage. Partnerships are built on trust. Without it, there is no foundation to stand on.

But what if you don't realize it? All this happened behind our backs. In those moments, the answer is the same: clarity. Our mistake was to give our initial partners *Certified Partner* badges once they completed their training. They loved it. Partners would brandish the badges on their websites, in email footers, and on business cards. But as a customer, you had no idea what it meant.

Because this was a pilot program, we did not mention our partners on our website. There was no info customers could find online. So the partners had to explain to each customer what the badge meant. This gave the bad actor an opening. Of course, they claimed they were an exclusive reseller. Of course, customers could only buy from them.

Soon after the incident, we implemented a fix. We added a partner directory to our website where we featured each partner agency. Again, partners loved it. They could show customers our website and say: "See, we're legit!" But even better, customers would read the description where we explained what it meant to be a partner. None of our partner agreements were exclusive. The customer could still buy from us directly. Clarity solves conflicts.

FROM 10 TO 1,000 SERVICE & CHANNEL PARTNERS

Once you've had a few successes with your initial partners, it's natural that your immediate thought is: How can we find more partners? Don't. It's always better to start small. At Hopin, we started with a group of 10 agencies for the first few months.[63] This was a blessing when issues occurred. Like when an agency took a sales rep's deal. We only had to update 10 agreements. It still took a lot of time, but it was manageable. The partners also knew they were part of a pilot program and changes could happen. Only when we were sure we found partner-market-fit did we scale to hundreds of partners.

There is another reason why it is smarter to start small. When Nelson Wang built the partner program at Box, he was quick to onboard over 700 partners.[64] He later realized that these were way too many partners. Why? If you have this many partners, chances are that many of them aren't very good. They don't align with your 4C's (Customers, Capacity, Capability, and Commitment). Worse, you might not have enough customers yet to support them. If you sign up 700 partners but only have 700 customers, at best you could send one customer to each partner. Pretty unappealing. If you only have 10 partners and 700 customers, each partner could service 70 customers. Very appealing.

On the flip side, this same logic is also the reason why you will want to scale your program eventually. Let's say you only have one partner who services all 700 customers of yours. What a dream, right? Only one agency to enable, one consultant to refer deals to, only one swim lane. But also, only one throat to choke when things go wrong. Classic *partner concentration risk*.

If you rely too much on one partner, things can get weird. Maybe they hold your customer's hostage and try to negotiate a large discount with you. Maybe they could raise prices on your customers because they have a monopoly on services for your product. Maybe their service quality deteriorates because "Hey, where else are these customers gonna go?" This is why a balanced partner portfolio is important. Some competition between partners is healthy. It encourages partners to offer the best service possible at the best prices. The customer wins so everybody else also wins.

When it is time to scale, two things become important: sourcing new partners and onboarding them into your program. We talked about finding partners at length. The only difference now is that you won't hold them by the hand anymore. Instead, partners should be able to self-select into your program. Make it easy for them to take your certification and join all by themselves. All you have to do is just nudge them with a link to your program.

Onboarding partners at scale, on the other hand, is less simple. Until now you might have gotten away with Fred-Flintstoning your onboarding and enablement. That's when you appear to have your act together on the outside, but pedal real hard behind the scenes to make things work. You can't do this anymore when hundreds of partners with dozens of employees each need to learn your tool.

You need a rock-solid certification program that any new partner employee can complete by themselves. Then you need automated workflows to make it easy for partners to register deals, ask for help, and stay up to date with your product changes.

In most books, this is the part where they lay it on you thick. "Buy our automation software! You need our partner relationship management software (PRM)!" I have no skin in the game. I don't make money if you buy one of these tools. I want you to win! So here's an unbiased opinion:

Backload any operations work as much as possible. Get the results first, then optimize. I have seen too many people waste the first few weeks on a new job on a lengthy PRM implementation or with complicated workflows. They frontload the operations work. Then, when they finally talk to partners, they realize that the tool doesn't do what they need. Or that it is set up for marketing partners but not channel sales. It's better to first talk to partners, make them win, and then optimize for scale.

Aaron Howerton, senior partner operations and experience manager at Samsara and a leading voice on partner operations, put it like this: "Delay any PRM implementation as long as humanly possible. You can do a lot with your partner network without a PRM. The problem is always that the PRM is here, but the CRM (customer relationship management software) is not ready for partnerships. When you bring your PRM too early and your CRM is not supporting your partnership team, you're wasting your time."[65]

Most startups don't have great data on their customers. Their CRM is often riddled with duplicates, missing information, or useless fields. If you then add another tool into the mix which pushes information to this hot mess of a CRM, you have a massive data problem. If you only have one CRM, you at least only have one steaming pile of chaotic data. With a PRM, you duplicate the mess in a separate location. There is a time and place for these tools, but you should be 100% sure you need them right now.

The same is true if you want to create a partner portal. An interface for your partners to log in to register deals, find enablement materials, and ask questions for your team. Antonio Caridad shared an important factor to consider here: "The average company has 30 partners. This means that your partner will have 30 different partner portals to log into, and 30 different interfaces. Hundreds of different workflows and ways to find information."[66]

Even if you think your partner portal is easy to use, it's one of 30 others your partner has to learn. They don't have time to study it. If it is just a little confusing, it will have a negative impact on your *partner experience* (PX). The sum of all the interactions a partner has with your company.

Initially, you as the partner manager are the PX. You have control over every interaction your partner has with your company. But as you begin to automate, things can get confusing. This is a big issue. Because your *partner experience* is your *customer experience* (CX). If partners think it is awful to work with you, they let your customers know. No matter what the issue, the partner will blame it on you. Your PX impacts your CX.

As your program grows, you will need to figure out a way to prioritize your partners. We discussed the *partner portfolio management* process in chapter 1. However, you will also need to find a way to communicate your priorities with your partners. There is only so much time in the day, so you need a way to explain to them how they are performing compared to other partners and what they need to do to get more of your attention.

One common mistake startups make at this stage is to create tiers for their partner program. Matt Bray, chief partnerships officer EMEA at SAP Signavio, shared why tiers don't make sense for startups.[67] Let's say your tiers are gold, silver, and bronze. Guess what. All partners will want to be platinum. Tiers only make sense if you have a large, well-established partner program. You need to know exactly what excellence looks like and how partners can achieve it. Then paint the path for them.

A more fun way to spark competition and rank partners is to create awards. Partners love to slap "award-winning agency" onto their website. Set metrics you care about, e.g., number of referrals made, implementation quality, or revenue generated. Then watch the competition unfold. Awards are a cheap, easy, and meaningful way to get your best partners to reach new heights. They also allow you to show your partner community what great looks like and reinforce the behaviors you want to see. Apart from a community milestone like a fun awards ceremony, you can also create case studies about the winners. Make the right partners famous and others will follow their playbook.[68]

CHAPTER 4:
PRODUCT PARTNERSHIPS

"Rather than thinking to build,
build to think."
—Tim Brown

INTEGRATIONS ≠ PARTNERSHIPS

"Ah yes, we have a partnership with HubSpot." I hear these words often when I talk to startup founders. When I then follow up and ask what kind of partnership, they seem perplexed: "Well, we integrate with them."

Here's the deal: An integration is not a partnership. Remember the definition:

A partnership is a relationship between two or more parties with the intent to create a competitive advantage.

Anybody can integrate with HubSpot. They have a public application programming interface (API). You can imagine it like a power outlet in a wall into which you can plug your product. This allows you to either send to or receive information from HubSpot. Anybody can plug into this API, so clearly there is no competitive advantage in an integration.

A *product partnership*, often also known as *tech partnership*, is the go-to-market wrapper around your integration. It is your *better-together-story*. All the activities you perform together to sell more and help customers achieve their goals.[69]

One great example of a product partnership is how PandaDoc, an e-signature startup, partnered with HubSpot, a customer relationship management platform (CRM).[70] Customers use HubSpot to track all their sales deals. PandaDoc had an integration with HubSpot, but that's not special. It would still have to find and convince each individual HubSpot customer to use their e-signature service to sign contracts.

The real partnership only happened when PandaDoc helped HubSpot discover a key insight: customers were 700% (!!) more likely to upgrade to a paid HubSpot license if they closed a sales deal. This made intuitive sense, but deals often got stuck in the signing stage. Back then, documents had to be printed, signed, sent, or photographed. It was a mess.

PandaDoc made this a lot easier and helped HubSpot convert a lot more customers from their free to their paid plans. Armed with this insight, PandaDoc's team was able to convince HubSpot to mention them in their product onboarding email. This is the first email new HubSpot customers receive. Tens of thousands of customers saw it every month.

Even better, they saw it at the right time: the moment they set up their CRM. This means PandaDoc was recommended to customers before they had a chance to consider other solutions. By the time a competitor reached out to the customer it was already too late. They had already picked their e-signature solution. That's the power of partnerships.

This story highlights a simple truth: Integrations are your defense, partnerships your offense. Imagine how PandaDoc would have approached HubSpot's customers, their target audience, without a partnership. A customer might be interested but say: "We can only use a solution that works with our CRM, HubSpot." PandaDoc would nod their head in excitement. The integration saved the deal. Hooray! But any other competitor like Hellosign or Docusign also has a HubSpot integration. They just didn't lose the deal to a competitor.

The partnership allowed them to get ahead of the competition. To avoid the side-by-side comparison a customer might make to choose their solution. To leverage the *social capital* HubSpot has built with their customers to nudge them to a product they trust. At least for that one specific but crucial use case: e-signatures.

The goal of a product partnership is to become the preferred solution of your partner for one specific customer problem. HubSpot could have built their own e-signature solution because a lot of customers needed one. But I am sure they went through their own *build, buy, partner decision* and realized it was not part of their core business. Better to focus on marketing automation and other areas they were good at. Partners can fill in the gaps and help you avoid *feature bloat*, which happens when your product becomes too complex and unusable.

Great product partners are a trusted extension of your product. We all love a mental shortcut. Customers don't want to browse dozens of e-signature tools. They want you to tell them which one works well with your solution. So you go out and vet a bunch of them and then tell your customers: "We like PandaDoc but also work with a whole list of other tools."

The customer will ignore the list because, who cares? They'll sign up with PandaDoc and you know your customers are in good hands. It's a win-win.

Apart from making more money, product partners also help you retain your customers. At Hopin, we found that customers who had installed at least three integrations were almost twice as likely to renew their contract compared to a customer who had not integrated our product into their toolstack at all.

The reason why is obvious when you look at the situation through the lens of our customers. It's one thing to switch your events platforms. But if you also have to change your interpretation tool, event registration page, and a whole list of other vendors, the risk is massive. We call this the *lock-in-effect*.

The team communication platform Slack has perfected this approach. At the previous startup I founded we felt the lock-in-effect in full force. First, Slack gets you started on a free plan. Then they encourage you to integrate your favorite apps. Finally, they send you a bill for several thousand dollars per month.

When this happened, we decided to move to a cheaper tool. But that same day, the engineers complained that the tool didn't have an integration with their task management tool, Jira. Then sales complained that the HubSpot integration was unstable. HR chimed in that our recruitment tool wouldn't sync. The next day, we were back on Slack.

There is one exception where an integration can create a competitive advantage: If you have exclusive access to it. This can happen in two ways. You can have such a strong partnership that your partner will open up an integration for you. For example, when LinkedIn wanted to roll out live streaming on their platform, they tapped StreamYard to be one of the first platforms to build their new API. In exchange, we provided their team with feedback and insights based on our extensive experience in the live streaming market.

This was technically just an integration, but because it was exclusive to our company you can be damn sure we told the whole market all about it. The engagement also opened up more opportunities to work with the LinkedIn team over time which led to LinkedIn even investing in our company.

ARE YOU READY TO BUILD?

Product partnerships can be very expensive. It can take weeks or even months to build an integration with a partner. A lot can go wrong during that time. I have built several integrations which never made it to market or flopped big time. If you are lucky, customers just don't use your integration. You wasted your team's time, but that's it. The worst case scenario is that customers want to use your integration but it does not work.

For example, at Hopin, this could mean that a customer hosts a huge event. They get tens of thousands of attendees to register through a partner. Then, on the day of the event, the organizer realizes attendees can't get into the event. If this ever were to happen, customers would be upset. Lawsuit upset. The cost of failure is so high, you have to get your integrations right.

You can also build integrations without a product partnership. Without a go-to-market wrapper around them. At Hopin, we had integrations with all major CRMs. But we only partnered with two. When Salesforce asked us to join their partner program, we politely declined. Our ideal customers sat in the marketing team, which was more likely to use marketing tools like HubSpot and Marketo. It made no sense for us to partner with Salesforce. However, customers still wanted to export data to their CRMs, so we built an integration to be defensive.

Any product partnership needs to be a deliberate decision by your team. Yet too often partnerships teams make emotional calls like "Oh look, an email from a potential partner." They then dream up a grand vision of how awesome it would be to use your two products together. A classic *Barney partnership*.

Why? Because they forgot to ask the most important stakeholder in the *partner value triangle*: the customer. Instead, your discovery process should always start from the customer's perspective:

1. What problems do our customers need to solve?
2. What do your customers' current workflows look like?
3. What tools do they use to solve these problems?

The order here is important or else you might end up with the wrong partnership. I mentioned that back in 2021 we had a flopped integration with a crypto company because the partner wasn't ready for prime time. Bummer, but at least there technically was demand for the integration.

Around the same time, we also had a set of customers who were obsessed with the metaverse. They wanted something futuristic to add to their events. Avatars, intricate 3D models, "virtual serendipity." The problem was that no customer could point to a specific product they wanted to use. They liked the idea of the metaverse but wanted us to pick a partner who could bring it to life.

I had learned from my crypto mistake. This time I would find a partner who was enterprise ready. But when the integration rolled out, customers didn't want it. Too expensive. Too complicated. The vibes were off.

Repeat after me: Unless you have shared customers, you are shooting in the dark. Don't chase vague trends in partnerships. The risks are too high. You need conviction and evidence that customers want what you are building. So the goal at this stage is to gather data points on a problem or workflow customers need help with. Ideally, you also have a short list of potential partners your customers already work with to solve their problems.

The best way to get an initial read is to jump on customer calls. Ask them to walk you through their workflows. Record these calls. Understand how they use your product. What are their *jobs-to-be-done?*[71] Not the tasks they want to perform, but the outcomes they want to achieve through those tasks? This process is called *customer discovery*. If you want to do it right, I highly recommend you read *The Mom Test* by Rob Fitzpatrick.[72]

Qualitative user feedback will often not be enough to convince your most important internal stakeholder: your product team. This team will have done their own research that you can plug into. But chances are that they will look at everything through a product lens. "We have a product hammer, so all issues fall into the "build" quadrant of our *build, buy, partner strategy*."

Most people's knee jerk reaction to this problem is to put a "request integrations" form up on your website. This way they can collect customer requests for new integrations and show some real data. It's a start, but not great. Only a fraction of all customers will complete this form. A lot of them also might not even realize their workflows can be improved.

Xiaofei Zhang, director of platform and strategic Partnerships at ActiveCampaign, shared a better hack: Add a search bar to your partner page. Then track what customers search for.[73]

Ideally these customers are logged into your product, so you know who they are. But even if you don't, you will get a lot more insights from their searches than any form. There's a reason Google is such a huge business! Searches tell you what people really want.

Another great source of insights is your customer facing teams. Sales, support, customer success. Get your team to commit to asking: "What tools do you use together with our product?" Then collate their feedback. You could get them to enter this information into a dedicated field in your CRM. But this is painful. It becomes much easier if all customer calls are recorded using a sales intelligence tool. These tools transcribe meetings, look for keywords, and then send you a report on how often certain partners were mentioned. Nice.

Andrew Edelman, former director of platform & strategic partnerships at Zapier, shared another great hack for software startups: Instead of guessing which integrations your customers want to use, let them tell you. You can do this through an iPaaS (*integration-platform-as a-service*) solution like Zapier. These tools have built integrations with 6,000+ products already. All you have to do is integrate with the iPaaS. One integration, and your customers can connect 6,000+ tools with your product! You then look at what are the most popular tools customers connect with. E voila! You have your short list.

There is a catch though. Your product team won't like this type of "middleware." It's a black box that sits between your two products. Neither you nor your partner have control over it. Enterprise customers don't like middleware either. They see it as another point of failure. And small customers often dislike it, too. "Great, another thing we need to set up!" They also have to pay for it. But, hey, it's better than no integration at all. Middleware is a great defensive move to cover your bases.

At Hopin, we would often pay for a customer's Zapier license in exchange for a customer case study about our *better-together-story* with a new partner. This way we could test out whether we needed a proper integration and if a product partnership made sense. We also had our first partner marketing materials and a happy customer. Win-win-win.

THE INTEGRATION NEGOTIATION TANGO

With your shortlist in hand and your product team's sign off on your *build, buy, partner decision,* it is time to vet your partners. Remember the *4C's of Partnerships* we discussed in chapter 1. We already mentioned the importance of customers and credibility, but when it comes to product partnerships you need to pay special attention to two other areas: Capabilities and Commitment.

Capabilities: Product partnerships are very involved. You not only work with your partner's product team, but also their sales, marketing, and support teams. There is a lot that can go wrong. Especially on the product side.

One morning, I noticed one of our integrations broke. Our customers noticed, too. In fact, the partner's entire website was down. Everybody freaked out. The partner sent me a panicked message: "You need to update our integration ASAP!"

Here is what happened: Many years ago, the founder paid for the company's website domain with his personal credit card. Sure, he was just a guy in his apartment with a random idea. Now he runs a 100+ people company. But the $9.99/year payment was never moved to a business card. When his credit card expired, the payment failed. The company's domain was up for sale! Within seconds a domain squatter snatched it away! Now, some random person held the domain of a multimillion-dollar company hostage!

Not only were the startup's own customers screwed. Their partners and their customers were, too. All because of their incompetence. This is an extreme case, but it often happens that partners mess up an integration. I have seen this especially when the partner hires a software development shop in Eastern Europe to build an integration. Yes, you save money by outsourcing your work. But you pay dearly with your *social capital*.

It is expensive to hire and train the right people to build up your capabilities. But given the large impact product partnerships can have on your business, you have to put your best foot forward at all times. You can always raise more money from VCs. But *social capital* is far harder to earn.

Commitment: Another big issue with product partnerships is how resource intensive they are and how long they take. This can lead to partners with commitment issues. You might be able to convince a partner at first. But once the real work starts, they chicken out. Like your first boyfriend when you asked him to move in with you.

The secret to successful product partnerships is to not rely on one single point of contact. Instead, you have to build a *coalition of support*. A group of people at both your own and the partner company who rally around the partnership. These will have to include at least one product leader, but also sales, marketing, support, or executives. Any team whose help you might need to make the partnership a success.

This process is also called *multi-threading a relationship*. Like a steel cable, you weave together individual strands of relationships until you form an unbreakable bond between your companies. It is the only way I have found to ensure your partnership survives in the long run. People will always leave a company at some point, but this shouldn't derail your partnership. Your goal is to transcend individual people and make sure you align with the goals of the company as a whole. Plus, each individual team.

Once you have identified your partner shortlist, rallied your team, and vetted your partners, a curious phase begins: *the integration tango*.

The negotiation around a product partnership is different from any of the previous types of partnerships we discussed. There the roles are more clear cut. You build the product, and a service partner provides services around it. Easy. In a marketing partnership, you both promote each other's products. Also easy.

For product partnerships there are two different tasks though: building and promoting the integration. Often, both partners could build the integration. More often than not, neither side wants to. Integrations are expensive and hard. At least on the surface, promotion seems far easier.

This makes intuitive sense. Engineers get paid more than marketers. But unfortunately, you can't both build half of the integration and do half of the promotion. That's not how products work.

Dan Rose, former VP of partnerships at Facebook, also thinks this is a bad idea :"A 50/50 split leaves everybody unhappy. Good partnerships maximize value for both sides with minimal waste. If you are bargaining over an orange, one resolution is to slice it in half. But if you dig deeper into the motivations of each side, you might find one party cares about the meat while the other cares about the rind."[74]

Let me break it to you though: If you are a tiny startup, your partner will take the meat and the rind. You will have to build AND promote any integration. This is why it is so important for startups to be smart about their product partnerships. Even if you do all the work for the partner, there still needs to be some juice to squeeze.

Nevertheless, there are some tactics you can use to master the *integration tango*. Francois Grenier, former head of partnerships at Typeform, shared his secret: "You have to be in the 'quick wins' quadrant for all your partners."[75]

His key insight at Typeform was that partners will build with you if you're the easiest company to build with. Francois' team obsessed about the developer experience the way founders obsess about their customers. They leverage Typeforms' well-known brand to create a menu of marketing resources they could dangle in front of partners. To seal the deal, he also presented his partners with historic usage data they could use to convince their internal teams to build the integration. All these efforts paid off. Typeform had 100+ integrations, of which they only built 28 themselves.

Christine Li, VP of global partnerships at G2, shared another important tactic with me on a podcast: "Always align yourself with the KPIs (key performance indicators) of the partner's product team."[76] It doesn't matter if your partnership counterpart is on board. Their product team holds the keys to the engineering resources they need to build the integration. Figure out what the product team's priorities are and how you can help them win. If done well, even a David might get a Goliath to build an integration for them. And Christine knows what she's talking about. Her team convinced giants like Amazon Web Services and Microsoft to build a G2 integration!

G2 is the #1 software review site in the world. It is home to millions of vetted and trusted reviews on all sorts of software products. Remember the SWOT analysis? Trust was her team's greatest strength. After discussions with the product teams at AWS, Microsoft, and SAP, Christine discovered a major insight: The companies had thousands of integrations in their app marketplaces. Yet customers didn't leave reviews about these partners. Since most apps had no reviews, other customers couldn't decide which partner app to buy and integrate. Fewer integrations means lower product usage by the customer and a higher risk of churn.

Armed with this insight, G2 developed a "review syndication API" which would cross-post reviews from G2 onto partner marketplaces like the AWS marketplace. At first, Christine decided to offer the API for free. Partners didn't want it. But then something incredible happened: She decided to charge partners for the API and adoption skyrocketed.

Why? "There needs to be some form of upfront commitment." Christine explained. "If no money changes hands, nobody talks about the investment." Through a price tag, Christine got her partners to consider the value of this integration. Yes, she had to sell the vision, but once the deal was inked there were no more commitment issues during the build phase.

Somebody at her partner company put their neck on the line to secure the budget for this integration. This person was now accountable for the return on investment. They had to see the integration through. Ask your partners to show their commitment somehow. Marketing resources, money, time with their engineers. Anything. Make it hurt if they don't follow through.

Another way to get commitment is to put dollar amounts on your integration. Or euros, if you drink your cappuccino only before noon. The two main considerations when you calculate the return on investment of an integration are 1) cost of the integration and 2) the money you will make or save.

Ryan Lunka, CEO of Blended Edge, expressed these factors in a simple formula:[77]

Return On Investment

$$= \frac{(Revenue\ Acceleration + Cost\ Savings) - Cost\ to\ Develop + Cost\ To\ Maintain)}{Cost\ to\ Develop + Cost\ to\ Maintain}$$

As you can see, the cost of an integration is not only its development. Maintenance is the real issue that is often overlooked. APIs change. Customers will request new features. Somehow, something always breaks. That's why integrations are difficult. It is one thing to sell your team on a one-off project. It's another to burden them with ongoing, often random and urgent customer support for the integration. As you add more integrations, maintenance can bog down your team. To calculate these numbers, you need:

Cost to develop = # engineers × # hours spent on the integration × $ per hour

Multiply all these numbers. Then double them. Integrations always take longer than expected. You also need to add in an estimated opportunity cost. These engineers won't be able to work on other projects. Since engineers are expensive, this number tends to be quite large. This is by design. Product partnerships are not for the fainthearted. You need a rock-solid business case.

As you noticed, calculating the cost of an in-house integration is a bit fluffy. One way to get a concrete number is to hire an external developer or agency to build and maintain the integration for you. This comes with its own challenges. Nick Valluri, director of strategic partnerships at Dropbox, shared that incentives for agencies are often not aligned with your goals. If they are paid a fixed amount, like $100,000 for an integration, they will try to rush the job. There's no point in spending more time on it than needed. They actually benefit if the integration is poorly built. It will break more often, which means a recurring stream of maintenance revenue for the agency.[78]

Outsourcing your integration work is not all awful, of course. You don't have to worry about opportunity cost because your product team is less hands on. These dev shops are also often located in low-cost countries, which means you might get the job done cheaper and quicker. Just be sure to ask your network for recommendations to agencies they trust.

On the revenue side, two factors are important: cost savings and revenue acceleration. We already know that it is often cheaper to partner than to build features in-house.

Your product team can help you put a number on this using the same formula as above.

Nick then recommends you enlist your sales team for help.[79] This team feels the pain of a missing integration the most. In an ideal world, sales keeps track of all the deals they lost. Like prisoners who track their days with chalk on the wall of their cells: $50 thousand lost to a competitor due to a lack of integration, $100 thousand lost to a competitor, $25 thousand lost.

This frustration makes them the ideal internal champions for your integrations and product partnerships. Unfortunately, this team is often too busy. They need to close deals. No time to keep track of anything. So it is often on you to pull together all the pieces you need to create a business case. How many deals did we lose in the past? How many more will we win in the future?

If the ROI of your integration is above three, you are in business. If it's lower than one, you expect to lose money on this integration. Anything in between will depend on your judgment. Is this integration strategic? Are there positive knock-on effects not mentioned in the formula? Whatever it is, write it down. Inevitably, six months down the line, you will have a team retrospective meeting where somebody will ask: "Why did we do this again?"

As you craft your business case and negotiate with partners, there is one cheeky tactic that all partner managers use but never talk about: Inflate the effort of the activities you have to offer. It works like this: You negotiate activities with your partners and make them sound as painful as possible. "Build an integration? This will take us months! A press release? Our PR team will rip my head off!" Then you find easy ways to deliver these things in the background.[80]

For this tactic to work you will have to create two business cases: an exaggerated one you show your partner. And one actual business case for internal use. Your partner will be incentivized to stretch themselves and commit to more activities. Your team, on the other hand, will be able to deliver far faster than the partner expects. Under promise and over deliver.

One way to do this is to have a set menu of marketing activities that you negotiated with your marketing team in advance. Pair this with a commitment from your team to allocate a certain number of social posts, blogs, and webinars to your partners each month. Now, after a painful negotiation, all you have to do is turn around and ping your marketing team. Easy.

The same is true for integrations. It really does take weeks or months to write code for them. As we discussed, there are also unknown maintenance costs. Middleware is often disliked, but there is a middle ground (no pun intended).

Some iPaaS providers allow you to set up their platform so that everything happens behind the scenes. Customers often can't tell that the integration is based on an iPaaS. The downside is that your team still has to configure each individual integration within the iPaaS. But some tools allow you to do this in a few days. Sure beats the time it takes to build every integration from scratch! Whether or not you should use an iPaaS depends on your product and the classic trade off: control vs. speed.

Once you've wrapped up the dance and have a list of activities both sides agreed on, a common issue is that either side can forget. A lot of time might pass between the build and promotion phase. You need an easy way to remind all stakeholders what they committed to.

A contract is okay, but you never want to be the person who whips out a huge contract at a meeting and says: "Ah, but on page 22, paragraph 6 you agreed to . . . " Nobody likes that person. Instead, partnership professionals capture all activities in your *memorandum of understanding (MOU)*. For startups, this document should never be longer than two pages. Personally, instead of a block of text, I prefer one simple slide with three columns:

Memorandum of Understanding (MOU)		
Product	**Marketing & Services**	**Terms & Conditions**
What should the integration do? What features are in scope? This is important to avoid *scope creep*—when somebody slips in random requests that delay the whole timeline.	What marketing activities has each side committed to? How many impressions do we expect to generate with each activity? Who is responsible for internal and external enablement around the integration?	All details that will govern the partnership, like: • *Service level agreement (SLA)* • Expected timelines • Revenue share* • IP ownership* • Break clauses • Financials* • And more *If applicable

Fig. 10: Partnership Memorandum of Understanding (MOU) Template.

The MOU is crucial to ensure all sides are on the same page. Product partnerships often involve dozens of people. There needs to be a simple document an executive, but also somebody in customer support, can pick up and say: "Ah, I get it!" Another reason why you don't want to jump into a contract straightaway is that the terms might change dozens of times. The MOU slide strips away all the legal noise. Only when everybody signed off on your MOU slide should you hand it to your lawyer to translate it into an agreement. Saves you plenty of expensive lawyer hours.

Often an executive at either company will ask for a business plan. In my experience, this is a waste of time. This isn't university! You don't get points for writing complicated 20-page essays that nobody reads. Any document you create should be simple enough to review on a regular basis. Daniel O'Leary, senior director of partnerships at Box, therefore prefers to create a *joint success plan*.[81]

Daniel came up with the idea for *joint success plans* after he joined dozens of calls with his customer success team. At Box, customer success managers create plans together with each new client on how they can make them successful. This is when it clicked: "Partners are just customers in disguise," he told me during our podcast interview.

These plans are crucial because they make sure that each side allocates the necessary resources to make the partnership a success. You can't have a $10 million partnership unless you put in a $10 million effort! To create a joint success plan, all you have to do is divide up your MOU:

- Who is in charge of which activity?
- What resources will they need?
- When will it happen?
- What outcome do we expect from it?

That's it. Sounds simple, right? It's not. Again, incentives and time kill partnerships. Because product partnerships take a long time to complete, incentives can shift. Crypto currencies were all the rage in 2021, but in 2022 not so much. So you can expect that the product team's excitement may have also waned.

To get ahead of these issues, Daniel recommends you treat your *joint success plans* as a living document. Every month, review the plan together with your partner. Understand how their *SWOT analysis* has changed. What new opportunities or threats have emerged? More importantly, have they changed their *build, buy, partner strategy*? New activities. Shifting priorities. Extended deadlines. Everything has to go into the plan.

If there are issues, you better know about them early. As Benjamin Franklin puts it: "If you fail to plan, you plan to fail." Or Daniel's updated version: "You plan the work and then you work the plan."

CO-SELLING STRATEGIES WITH PRODUCT PARTNERS

Co-selling is where the rubber hits the road. It is the go-to-market wrapper around your integration that turns it into a true product partnership. This is important because otherwise partnerships are a bit fluffy. We assume that our relationships with other companies help, but we can't put a finger on it. When you co-sell with a partner, that indirect influence turns into undeniable sales revenue. Cold, hard cash. If implemented well, your deals will close faster, win rates are higher, contract values increase, and customers will be retained for longer.

Co-selling is enabled by co-marketing, which we discussed earlier in this book. The main difference is the depth of the partnership. At this stage, you strengthened your *better-together-story* with an integration. But it's not enough to list your integration on your partner's app marketplace and lean back. "Build it and they will come" never works.

It is time to jump into the trenches with your partner's customer-facing teams. You will have to go after individual sales deals. This takes a lot of time and effort, so the most important aspect is to figure out which integrations deserve to become product partnerships.

Alyshah Walji, director of partnerships at Vividly, recommends that we look at our data for clues.[82] What do all your existing customers have in common? How can we find more customers like them?

The key insight here is that your product tends to attract a certain type of customer. One way to define this type of customer is through the other product they use. No customer uses your tool in isolation. Whether by change or by design, your product will often be optimized to work well with another partner's tool.

At this stage it's important to remember that the *SaaS Buying River* dictates your co-marketing partnerships.[83] The same principle applies here. Think through your customers' buying journey: When they knock on your door, what tools have they already bought? What other tools will they need after they buy yours?

If they already bought a competitor's tool, it will be hard to get them to rip and replace it. The best co-selling opportunities are with partners whose customers haven't bought a tool like yours yet. Look upstream if you want to generate revenue from co-selling with partners. Look downstream if you want to co-sell partner tools into your customer base to make your customers "stickier" or increase usage.

There is another reason you need to be picky about your partners: compound interest. Product partnerships are a long-term strategy. The more joint customers you have, the more success stories you create. In turn, you will attract more customers and have a greater incentive to improve your integration. This virtuous cycle can catapult your entire company forward as long as the partner's customer base is large enough to sustain your growth for years to come.

Once you identify the right partners to co-sell with, get specific about which customers you want to tackle together. In his book *Ecosystem-Led Growth,* Bob Moore shares the three types of customers you can co-sell to with your partner:[84]

- **Joint opportunities:** a new customer for both you and your partner. In this case your "better together" story helps you create a competitive advantage to win a joint deal.
- **Your opportunity is a partner's customer:** leverage partner intelligence, relationships, and

advice to increase your speed and chances for winning a deal in your pipeline.

- **Your customer is a partner's opportunity:** help partners cross-sell into your customer base, increasing feature adoption and making your existing clients "stickier" thanks to the "better together" value story.

There are three ways partnerships can help you close these opportunities: intel, influence, and introduction.[85]

Who were the decision makers on your deal? How did you approach pricing negotiations? What did the customer care about? The right intel and partner gossip will make your prospect think you can see inside their head. Your pitch will be so tailored to the customer's needs, your competitors will look like amateurs going in blind.

Influence refers to the good words or case studies a partner can share with your prospect to sway them in your direction. You leverage the trust and *social capital* the partner has built with their customers to influence their decision making.

If you play your cards well, the right intel and influence can result in an introduction to your target customer. This is a moment of maximum tension. The partner expends significant *social capital* and vouches for you. You need to bring your A-game and deliver every time to avoid *relationship debt*.

So far so good. Here's the hard part: How do you know if you have a shared customer or opportunity with a partner? In the olden days, you would print out a list of all your customers. Meet the partner in a dingy, smoke-filled room with a single, low-hanging lamp. Then you smoke Marlboros and compare lists. Glorious, but sketchy. Too much information is being shared. This was clearly before GDPR, the data protection law of the European Union.

These days, there are plenty of ways to identify shared opportunities: account mapping tools like Crossbeam allow you to connect to only share customers who fall into one of the three buckets mentioned above. The rest are kept secret. Other customer intelligence tools allow you to type in a customer's website and see their entire tool stack.

However, partnerships are a people business. Technology can help us optimize our workflows, but it can't replace the hard work that goes into building trust and *social capital*. So instead, we will focus on the core process of co-selling with a partner without leveraging partner tech for now.

Olga Lykova, head of North America partnerships at monday.com, shared a playbook she used to drive 50 to 80% of revenue at companies like Workspot and Apttus. Without partner tech, but a lot of elbow grease and a relentless focus on her customer and partner experience.[86]

The first step is to identify your *buzzwords*. These are trigger words that answer this question: When should a partner team member think of you? As we discussed in the co-marketing chapter of this book, you have to pick your niche within your partner's ecosystem. You won't be relevant to all their customers. Buzzwords help your partner's team identify if a customer is a good fit for you during conversation. Live streaming? Think StreamYard. Quote-to-Cash? Apttus. Virtual Events? Hopin. Customer starts a call with "Guten Tag"? German service provider.

Once you have identified your niche and buzzwords within the partner ecosystem, you can train their team to look for those terms. This can be during current conversations with customers, or historical ones. You can either filter through call notes manually or use sales intelligence tools like Gong or Chorus. These tools record all customer calls and make it easy to set up keyword filters. Whenever somebody mentions a partner buzzword, the partner manager on the team gets a ping.

However, integrations aren't always the first thing customers think about when they want to buy your tool. So to set them and yourself up for success, you need to ensure that questions about the customer's tool stack and service providers are part of every discovery and onboarding call. This increases the chance that a customer drops a buzzword, and you can identify a joint opportunity.

The goal here is to stay top of mind for your partners and be remembered in the right moments. Buzzwords tend to work the best because they trigger a memory of you in the right moment. But there are other, more unconventional options, too. Cory Snyder, former head of partnerships at Sendoso, increased the number of referrals he received from a partner by 500% through one simple trick.[87]

Cory sent a small succulent to every single customer success manager at the partner company. All 200 of them! Referrals instantly shot up. Why? Because most people placed the succulent on their desk. Every time they looked at it, they thought of Cory and Sendoso. This hack worked especially well because Sendoso is in the gift-sending business. How can you stay top of mind for your partner teams?

The second step is to identify and build up your *champions*. These are people who are enthusiastic and eager to engage with you or a partner. They want to learn more and spread the word about the partnership within their organization. The idea of a champion is important because the biggest mistake partner professionals make when it comes to co-selling is to try to enable everybody.

They assume that after one lunch and learn session, their entire team will understand the in's and out's of the partnership and be excited to pitch them to their customers. This is unrealistic. Just think about how long it takes to onboard your own salespeople? Nobody will understand your entire product after a thirty-minute session while they're stuffing a burrito in their face. People have a lot going on. They have their own product to sell. There are dozens of other partners who want their attention. How can you stand out?

The answer, as always, is results. Find a small group of champions and make them really, really successful. Pour all your efforts into them. Be their quarterback who sets them up for success. But don't place all your eggs in one basket. Otherwise, your champion might leave the business and all your efforts are wasted.

How do you identify champions? Olga Lykova shared that they are often hiding in plain sight: "Anybody at a partner company who reaches out to you and asks for more information is a potential champion." These people often have an existing need for your solution. Learn more about them and their customers. How can your tool help? Then ask them for introductions to other potential champions.

This shouldn't be an excuse to sit and wait for people to ask questions. Instead, find ways to start conversations. I joked about lunch & learn sessions, but team enablement is a great way of identifying excited champions who want to engage. Just don't treat these sessions as the end of your enablement efforts. They are the start.

You can also ask your partner counterpart for introductions to people who are relevant to your business. In the chapter on channel sales, we talked about partner swim lanes. Similarly, most sales and customer success teams have swim lanes. People who focus on a certain geography, industry, or company size. Find the people who are most relevant to your product. Then make them really successful. Once they crush their sales quota, others will take note and want to co-sell with you as well.

The last step is to be the easiest partner to work with. This can mean many things, so you will need to uncover what the different partner sales teams need from you. One of the most common issues Olga flagged is that team members often don't know how to reach you.

One easy fix is to have a partnership specific email address, like partnerships@hopin.com. This email address should be monitored by all relevant parties, so you don't miss a customer introduction due to time zones or vacations. For large, strategic partners you can also easily flatter them with a custom address like google@yourcompany.com.

Now imagine you are a sales rep on your partner's team. You hung up on a call where a customer mentioned your buzzword like "virtual events," and you want to introduce them to a partner. Because you don't have a strong opinion, you reach out to three different partner companies in this space and ask for more information. Who do you pick?

Often, the answer is simple: the fastest. You want your deal to move along quickly. You copy and paste the information of whomever responds to you first. Then you're onto your next deal. This is the insight that helped Olga win 50 to 80% of her companies' revenue through partnerships.

To ensure they are the fastest partner every single time, she and her team instated an internal 10-minute response SLA (service level agreement). Every time a partner reaches out, she responds within 10 minutes. This is incredibly hard to do and takes a lot of preparation. You will need template emails, easily accessible slide decks and one-pagers, and a cooperative team monitoring your shared inbox. But the results speak for themselves.

As we discussed before, if you are waiting for a partner to respond, you are doing it wrong. The best partner managers are proactive. Inbound opportunities can be quick wins. But you will have to pedal hard to spin the flywheel. Go get those early wins.

The amateur move here is to straight up ask a partner: "Who could you introduce me to?" I've seen many partners take this approach and it leads nowhere. You are asking me to do all the work! Why would your partner want to figure out who could be a great customer for you?

Instead, Marco De Paulis, former head of partnerships at logistics giant Ryder, recommends that you have to make the first move. Send your partner a deal.[88] Show them you can provide value. All humans want to reciprocate, so they will be more inclined to help you score a win as well.

Now, with a warmed-up relationship, you can ask your partner for a customer introduction in return. Alyshah Walji shares that this usually fails in two ways: The partner doesn't know who to introduce you to. Or the customer they introduce you to says no.[89] Both situations suck. Both can be avoided.

Successful referrals have to be planned. You need to do your research. Which of your partner's customers do you want an introduction to? How does your product solve an issue for this customer? Why is now the right time for an introduction? Specificity builds credibility. The more detailed your request, the more confidence your partner counterpart has that the customer wants to be introduced. Sales expert Sam McKenna calls this approach "Show Me You Know Me (SMYKM)." Show your partner and their customers that you've done your homework.

It doesn't stop here. Make it as easy as possible for your partner to introduce you to their customer. This often means that you have to write emails or text messages for them. A large part of the job of a partnership leader is to write content for others. Remove friction wherever you can. Engineer serendipity.

TURN YOUR PARTNER PROGRAM INTO AN ECOSYSTEM

Partner managers often get blinded by large numbers: Your competitor has an app store with 5,000+ integrations. Salesforce has 74,000+ certified consultants and implantation partners. How will you ever catch up? In reality, it's quite easy. Here's the secret:

A small number of partners generate the bulk of all revenue and app installs. When a company brags about a large volume of partners, it's safe to assume that most of them are inactive. Failed startups, in-house built apps, 1-to-1 integrations, one-off projects. The list goes on.

"Yeah, that's the *80/20 rule*, also known as *the Pareto principle, right?*" you might think. No. This would assume that out of 1,000 partner apps, 200 generate 80% of activity. It's far more extreme. The Top 1% of rich people in the world own almost 50% of all the wealth. Sounds unfair? Partnerships are even more unequal!

Think about your smartphone. In 2022, Sensortower analyzed the downloads of the most popular 900,000 apps on the Apple App Store and Google Play Store.[90] These apps were downloaded 87 billion times in 2022 alone. How many downloads do you think the top 1% of apps accounted for? The answer is 79%. The top 9000 apps were downloaded 72 billion times. In comparison, the bottom 99%, or 891,000 apps, were downloaded 15 billion times. Two developers, Meta and Google, generated more than 1 billion downloads each. That's 2% of all downloads from just two partners.

At Hopin, we saw a similar pattern play out. Our top five integrations generated more than 90% of the customer installs. This is great news for you as a partner professional. It doesn't matter if your competitor has 1,000 integrations. All you have to do is find the 10 products that really matter to your customers. Then partner with them. A lot.

Even better news: These few partners will often be market leaders in their field. Why? Because so many of your customers love them. Their products must be awesome. So a lot of other customers will also flock to them. This gives you an amazing playbook for partner recruitment:

1. Partner with the tool your customers most want you to work with.
2. Make this partner really, really successful.

3. The partner's competitors will freak out and flood your inbox.
4. Then make it easy for your partner's competitors to build integrations.

Congratulations! You now developed integrations with every important company for one specific customer use case. There was no need to build all these integrations yourself. All it took was one, well-managed product partnership. Like the PandaDoc and HubSpot partnership earlier in this chapter. When HubSpot sent PandaDoc thousands of customers, other e-signature companies must have freaked out. I bet HelloSign and Docusign built integrations with HubSpot as soon as they could.

While they won't drive as many installs, these integrations are still important. First of all, they are free because the partner built them. Nice. Also, because you poured so much effort into your initial product partnership with the market leader, chances are your first integration is really good. This sets a high benchmark for all other competitor integrations. Even better!

Those additional integrations also helped create a defensive moat around your business. In HubSpot's case, some customers probably wanted to use HelloSign instead of PandaDoc. So it was still important to have integrations with both. And finally, competitors keep your main partner on their toes. While it is great to pick a winner, some level of competition among partners is crucial. Otherwise, you could face *partner concentration risk*.

I ran into this issue at Hopin with our interpretation partners. At first, we only had one partner for this use case. They made a killing. But soon after we started to get complaints from customers. Turns out the partner decided to raise their prices. By accident, we gave them a monopoly on interpretation services for Hopin customers!

We could have tried to fix this issue through a better contract. But every capitalist knows that the best antidote to a monopoly is not regulation. Competition is. We had a second interpretation partner waiting in the wings. They went above and beyond to win us over. As soon as they were onboarded, the service of both partners improved while prices went down. This was great for our customers. In turn, they hosted more virtual events on Hopin and bought more interpretation services. Win-win-win.

So far, we've talked a lot about how to manually onboard new partners. There is a flaw in this approach. You might miss some great opportunities because they looked small. Additionally, the strength of the best product partner programs comes from their diversity. There is an app for everything!

That's why you will eventually need to find a way to onboard all those smaller partners and custom integrations requests that customers send your way. Since each one of these integrations tends to be low value, but they become valuable in aggregate, the only way to cater to these partners is to build a self-serve developer platform.

This type of portal allows anybody to access your API documentation and a developer environment to build their own integrations. As Chris Saad, former head of product for Uber's Developer Platform, framed it: "You don't need to pre-qualify partners if you open up the platform and let developers experiment and iterate in a safe way. Apple didn't prequalify Instagram or Uber. They were emergent and unexpected outcomes of the curated but open platform."[91]

The benefits of an open platform are obvious. In the beginning, Steve Jobs wasn't a fan of an app store where partners can build their own apps. Apple would have never become the company it is today if he had tried to pick Instagram or Uber himself. If you have the resources to build a great program, you can let the market pick great winners for you.

As you add more product partners though, you will run into a common issue: You can't focus on all partners at the same time. A single partner manager can only balance so many relationships. Once the initial hype wears off, the romance starts to fade. Partners lose interest. They receive fewer leads from you, so they will put less effort into the partnership in return. It's a vicious cycle.

The best antidote is to mature from a two–directional partner program to an *ecosystem*. This term gets tossed around a lot, yet few people understand what it means. An ecosystem is a tight-knit web of companies that all interact with each other as part of a customer's workflows. The company at the center of an ecosystem is called the *supernode,* the holy grail of partnerships.

Partner Program **Ecosystem**

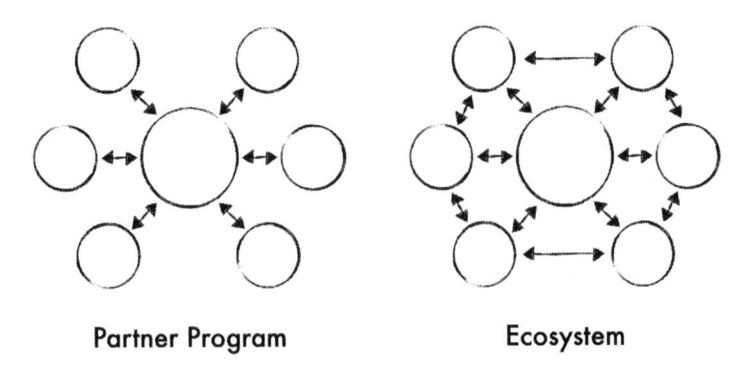

Fig. 11: The difference between a two-directional partner program and an ecosystem.
Source: Franz-Josef Schrepf

The difference between a partner program and an ecosystem is who interacts with each other. At the start, every partner will depend on your company for introductions, support, marketing, etc. As you add more partners, this becomes unsustainable. You only have so many hours in the day. So much good will with your marketing team. So much partner info your sales team can retain.

Instead, once you make your partners successful, the smart move is to introduce them to other relevant partners. When you connect your marketing, service, channel, and product partners with each other, magic happens. They will launch marketing campaigns together which focus on niche industries you never thought about. They will translate your sales deck into Hebrew and run localized sales plays for the Israeli market. They develop integrations with each other which make the customer's experience with your product even better.

The stronger the interactions between your partners, the more they will help each other win. Over time, the ecosystem will develop a life of its own. No need for you to interact with each individual partner on a regular basis. They will be too busy talking to each other and with your joint customers.

Because they perpetuate themselves, an ecosystem can be your business ultimate competitive advantage. It's how giants like Salesforce, Microsoft, and Shopify grew to such large sizes and managed to fight off the competition. Everything becomes easier: Channel partners source new customers for you and your other partners. Product partners will integrate with each other to create a seamless experience for your customers. Service partners will set up all of your customers' tools so they won't have to move a finger. The only thing customers have to feed into the ecosystem is money and all their business problems go away. Sadly, not their personal problems. Although I know at least one story where two partners got married. Nice.

The playbook above shows how you can build an *ecosystem* around your product, one vertical at a time. You probably noticed a flaw in this logic though. For the flywheel to spin, you need to be able to make your partners win.

Big time. Your partners will want you to send them a lot of customers. If you are a tiny startup which can count its customers on one hand, this isn't realistic.

As a result, these startups can't build an ecosystem. But here's the catch: While you think of yourself as the *supernode* of your own ecosystem, you are also one single node in another company's ecosystem.[92] That's why Jared Fuller, host of the *Partner Up Podcast* (renamed as the *Nearbound Podcast*), instead suggests what he calls the Partner Up Approach: "Your startup should not aim to create an ecosystem unless you have won the ecosystem of your most important partner."[93]

What does it mean to win a partner's ecosystem? You have to become their most important partner for your specific use case. Your solution has to be a critical part of their operating model. Every one of their sales, support, and customer success teams should know your name. Even their service and channel partners should mention you in the same breath as the partner tool. In short, you surround the partner. You have to form a *strategic alliance*.

CHAPTER 5:
ALLIANCES

"Give me a place to stand, and a lever long enough, and I will move [markets]."
— **Archimedes, if he worked in partnerships.**

HOW TO MOVE A MARKET

Partnerships give your startup leverage. They extend your reach, product, and services. What turns a partnership into a strategic alliance is how all-encompassing it is. Your goal is to win the partner company's entire ecosystem for your specific use case. To get your alliance partner to promote you to all their partners and customers. You are entering the champions league of partnerships. The stuff of legends. Where the goal is not to move product, but to move entire markets.

Alliances, or often also called *strategic alliances* or *strategic partnerships*, are a combination of many or all of the previous partnership types we discussed in this book. They are "bet-the-company" type decisions that offer exponential growth opportunities. Or they can kill your company. To illustrate the point, let's look at the alliance between Microsoft and OpenAI, the startup that won the AI use case within the Microsoft ecosystem.[94]

As we discussed before, Microsoft announced a strategic alliance and giant $10 billion investment in OpenAI, the creators of ChatGPT, in 2023. At the time, OpenAI was a small startup with a few hundred employees in San Francisco. Yet their flagship product, ChatGPT, had onboarded over 100 million users in less than two months! Its release kicked off an AI hype cycle and almost killed not one but two industry giants.[95]

Underneath the hype, OpenAI was in deep trouble. AI models have no moat.[96] The only way to stay ahead is to invest tons of cloud computing resources into training better models. But the launch of ChatGPT made a lot of noise. The former AI incumbent, Google, took note. If you aim for the king, you better not miss. Google was ready to use the full might of its Google Cloud and DeepMind research teams to catch up and outpace OpenAI.

OpenAI also suffered from a lack of distribution. As a startup, it relied on hype and virality to spread the word. But when the hype fades, then what? ChatGPT was the perfect feature, but not a product. It had the potential to kill Google search, but not if Google puts its own tool in front of billions of users first.

As we learned, urgency is one of the most important factors in a company's *build, buy, partner strategy*. OpenAI had no time to build computing resources and distribution channels itself. It had no money to buy them. It had to partner.

In business, the enemy of my enemy is my friend. Mutual competitors can create an incentive and urgency to partner up. Google was the enemy. Another giant, Microsoft, also had their eyes set on them.

For the past twenty years, Google had dominated the search engine business unchallenged. Its closest competitor, Microsoft Bing, stagnated at 9% market share. Just enough to claim Google didn't have a monopoly. But not enough to pose a threat. Microsoft needed to disrupt the whole search business. AI was the answer.

Microsoft had an abysmal track record in AI, though. Remember Clippy, the Word helper? Or Cortana, Microsoft's version of Siri? No? How about Tay, the Twitter bot who had to be shut down because it started to spew antisemitic slurs?[97] No major player had missed the AI boat as many times as Microsoft. Satya Nadella, Microsoft's visionary CEO, could no longer ignore the issue or hope to build AI in house. Its lack of AI capabilities had become an urgent threat, but also an opportunity.

OpenAI and Microsoft seemed like the perfect strategic alliance: Microsoft would invest a total of $13 billion into OpenAI. Technically, OpenAI could have taken outside money and paid for compute. But in exchange for exclusivity, OpenAI got favorable rates for Microsoft Azure's cloud hosting. No outside investor could provide this level of cost efficiency.

The "killer feature" of the alliance was Microsoft's distribution. OpenAI knew that ChatGPT is a feature, not a destination in itself. When added into all of Microsoft's products, it can meet users where they already are and unleash its full potential across endless real-world use cases. Microsoft's vast partner network would help evangelize OpenAI's products to billions of users across the world. In exchange, Microsoft could add cutting-edge AI capabilities across its entire product portfolio almost instantly. Microsoft also benefited from OpenAI's brand as the world leader in AI. Microsoft overnight became the hottest AI stock in the public market. Its stock price soared.

This type of partnership is often referred to as *original equipment manufacturer (OEM)* partnership. The term is somewhat outdated but still often used. It's a relic from a time when hardware manufacturers used components from partners inside their products. Unlike a standard supplier, an OEM partner is also advertised to the end customer. A famous example is the microprocessor company Intel which slapped its "Intel Inside" stickers onto products of 500+ manufacturers.[98] This strategy allowed Intel, a niche hardware manufacturer, to become a household name. Similarly, Microsoft's Bing search engine was now "powered by OpenAI."

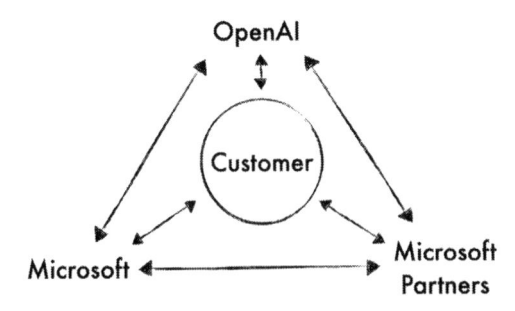

Fig. 12: Microsoft and OpenAI surrounded Microsoft's Customers. Source: Franz-Josef Schrepf, inspired by Jared Fuller.

Strategic alliances are the greatest lever a startup can wield. As Archimedes said: "Give me a lever long enough and a place to stand, and I will move the world." Strategic alliances don't move products, they move markets.[99]

The world witnessed one such move a mere two weeks after the alliance was announced in January 2023. Google rushed to announce its own AI chatbot, Bard. A total disaster. Executives rushed to hail Bard as the future of Google's entire search business. But the announcement video contained a factual error about who discovered an exoplanet. It was the type of issue anybody could have fact checked. You just have to google it.[100]

Google's stock price dropped by 9%. A whopping $100 billion was wiped off their market cap. Microsoft's stock, on the other hand, rose by 3% as investors expected them to integrate ChatGPT's superior capabilities into its Bing search engine. The strategic alliance shifted the entire search market into Microsoft's favor.

Or so it seemed. Microsoft committed the cardinal sin of partnerships: outsourcing a core capability. It is no understatement to say that the future of Microsoft depended on AI.

As we discussed before, core capabilities need to be brought in-house at all costs. They are too important to be left to third parties which you don't control. Especially not tiny startups which could pivot at a moment's notice. To make matters worse, OpenAI wasn't a normal startup. It was founded as a nonprofit organization to advance the creation of safe artificial general intelligence. The for-profit entity in which Microsoft invested was only added at a later stage. It was still controlled by the nonprofit arm and its board of independent directors. An awkward detail which almost killed Microsoft.

On November 17, 2023, out of nowhere, OpenAI announced that it had fired its CEO Sam Altman.[101] Microsoft had no seat on the nonprofit board. Their team had no idea what was happening. Overnight, the majority of the OpenAI team threatened to quit. OpenAI looked poised to implode. And along with it, Microsoft's entire AI strategy.

Microsoft tried to outsource a core capability in their *build, buy, partner strategy*. A mistake that could have been fatal. Ultimately, the crisis was averted, but Microsoft learned from its mistake. Soon after, it announced the creation of Microsoft AI, an in-house team dedicated to building its own AI capabilities. Much to the dismay of its partner, OpenAI.[102]

The Microsoft and OpenAI alliance is a prime example of the opportunities and threats strategic alliances can pose for your business. They are "kill the company" level decisions. You are dancing with elephants. It takes tremendous effort to set them in motion. You will need to channel all available resources you have to win their ecosystem. Yet their massive weight can crush you.

This is why strategic alliances have to be CEO-level decisions. If your partnership team is primarily focused on strategic alliances, then they should report directly up to the CEO. Given the strategic focus of this team on market expansion, people in charge of these alliances often have "Business Development" or "Strategic Alliance" in their title. They do this to create a separation from the other types of partnerships your company may have. This team needs unfiltered access to the CEO to help them rally every person within the organization behind an alliance. The company's future depends on getting these partnerships right.

There's something curious though about the Microsoft and OpenAI alliance: If artificial intelligence was a core activity for Microsoft but too urgent to build in-house, why didn't they buy OpenAI?

Startups often think that they have nothing to offer to industry giants. After all, these companies have unlimited resources and access to the world's top talent. They should be able to build or buy anything they want, right? Wrong.

Industry giants are bound by their own set of rules. As a startup looking to form an alliance, your job is to learn the rules by which the giant operates and play your cards to your advantage. In the case of OpenAI, their high-profile in the media and the perceived importance of AI meant Microsoft would have immediately been slapped with an antitrust lawsuit if it had tried to acquire them.

Instead, Microsoft had to settle for a 49% ownership stake. This allowed OpenAI to retain full control of its operation and product roadmap. A giant partner and full control. The best of both worlds. This setup also allowed OpenAI to enter into other strategic alliances, including with Microsoft's archenemy, Apple.[103]

Every giant operates by an unwritten playbook. Your job is to piece together this playbook and the context in which the giant operates. This will allow you to answer the most important questions in every alliance: Is there a real win-win opportunity?

Too often, startups are starstruck when an industry leader reaches out to them. "Google wants to partner with us?!" Immediately, the CEO rallies the entire company behind the "partnership with Google." And leads his team over a cliff.

Because you are dealing with giants, alliances are especially prone to the *shiny partner syndrome*. It is one of the reasons partnership teams have a bad reputation among executives. They prioritize big names and flashy logos over real business outcomes. These types of partnerships are almost always defensive: "We have to partner with Google, or else a competitor will!"

You have to stand up for what makes sense. Strategic alliances are "kill-the-company" type decisions. The cost of failure is too high to do something just to please your boss. Don't be afraid to say no. Even if it is your dream partner.

Vikram Ghosh, former SVP of strategic alliances at Secure Code Warriors, shared a simple rule of thumb: "One of the biggest people problems that we see, in terms of folks who are on point to build and drive alliances, is not raising the flag and saying 'Why are we doing this?' If they don't understand it and if you don't understand it, raise a flag."[104]

Otherwise, you will waste your own and your partner's resources on a partnership that is doomed to fail. Worse, news about the failure will incur *relationship debt* and make future partnerships harder. Maybe in this case you should be happy if your competitor leaps on the opportunity? It might hurt them and allow you to look for a better moment to engage.

If you are the business development leader at the larger partner, *shiny partner syndrome* is especially dangerous. Every startup you reach out to will want to partner. You must always ask yourself: Is this deal *partner-licious*? If you impose a bad deal on the startup, they will agree to it as a stepping stone to a potential larger partnership in the future. But over time, their excitement will fade. Resources will dry up. You might even kill their company.

Even if there is a *partner-licious* opportunity, another important factor to consider is timing. If your company is too small, a giant can crush you.[105] Strategic alliances are multiyear endeavors with a high rate of failure. They require high levels of patience and stamina. People love to overpromise and underdeliver. Big tech employees with cushy salaries are harder to move than hungry startup employees. Their onerous due diligence process can continue to reveal issues that need to be resolved. Priorities can shift and all your effort is wasted. Alliances can be a black hole for a startup's hopes, dreams, and funding.

Strategic alliances are a force multiplier for your startup. Yet you need to be able to stand on your own. Your startup needs to be able to generate revenue and survive even if the alliance fails. We call this state *default alive*. Otherwise, the process of setting up the alliance will break your neck.

This doesn't mean you shouldn't engage in conversations until you're ready. After all, are you ever really ready for anything? Mark Sochan, author of *The Art of Strategic Partnering: Dancing with Elephants,* still recommends startups to reach out to potential alliance partners right now.[106] Talk to the people who may be your partners one day. Your competitors sure are. It is impossible to guess when the right time for a partnership opportunity might arise. The best you can do is stay top of mind, so they remember you at the right moment. Just be aware that once you commit to an opportunity, your resource requirements will always escalate.[107]

Even if the right opportunity reveals itself at the right time, startups often make a big mistake: they are too ambitious. Sure, to get the attention of a company like Google or Amazon you need to promise a $50 million+ opportunity. It's still small fries, yet it'll turn some heads. But can you deliver? It's easy to say, "If Microsoft embeds our AI chatbot into all their products, we'll make a lot of money together." But this is also very risky for Microsoft. You might mess up!

How can you break the large vision into milestones you can use to de-risk the partnership? While Microsoft's giant investment and alliance announcement with OpenAI may have looked like a snap decision to many, in reality, it has been several years in the making. In 2019, Microsoft had invested $1 billion into OpenAI already.[108] At the time, OpenAI was only four years old with 100 employees. While still a sizable investment, it was a far cry from Microsoft going all in on OpenAI.

Over the following four years, Microsoft invested another $2 billion into OpenAI, until the release of ChatGPT rocked the world. At this point, the two companies already had five years of experience working together. They had built up the *social capital* to execute on a strategic alliance fast once the right opportunity arose.

A strategic alliance is like starting a whole new business within your company. This is the level of effort required to partner with giants. When Mark Brigman worked on a $5 billion alliance between the mobile network carrier Sprint and network infrastructure giant Ericsson, he was part of a 100-person team which coordinated the execution of the partnership.[109] A business within a business.

Fortunately, you don't need to be able to execute on your full vision tomorrow. Like a startup founder, your job is to paint the picture of the huge vision and opportunity for the alliance. Then lay out a series of steps you need to take to de-risk the alliance and reach your goals. Head in the clouds, feet on the ground.

WHICH ELEPHANT SHOULD YOU ASK FOR A DANCE?
It is hard work to identify the right elephant to dance with. Your company's future depends on it. Bernie Brenner, author of *The Sumo Advantage*, also describes why most CEOs are uncomfortable with this process. Alliances operate on a

multiyear time horizon. They're so far removed from the day-to-day challenges and quarterly numbers that nobody tends to think about them. You need to force the discussion.[110]

In an ideal world, every alliance discussion is centered around your customers. However, Bernie Brenner recommends that one way to immediately capture your executives' attention is to frame your alliance search around the competition: "What if our competitor partnered with X?" Strategic alliances are force multipliers. They can allow a competitor to leapfrog your company.

How did OpenAI know Microsoft was the right giant to partner with? Because in 2014, Google bought the London-based AI startup DeepMind.[111] This made Google unfit to partner, since it built most of its AI capabilities in-house. However, only a handful of other companies had the cloud-computing capabilities that OpenAI needed to scale: Microsoft, Amazon, and Oracle. Of these three players, Microsoft was the clear favorite. On top of its cloud computing capabilities, it also boasted over 345 million+ paid users for its Microsoft Office 365 suite.[112] It owned 46% of the office software market, compared to Google's 48%. This was the market OpenAI wanted to break into.[113]

While Amazon had a larger market share in cloud hosting, it could in no way rival Microsoft's distribution among business customers. This was OpenAI's best shot to outpace Google and DeepMind. Soon after the announcement of the deal, Amazon invested $4 billion in Anthropic, an AI startup founded by former OpenAI employees.[114] The table has been set. With the best partners snatched up, new entrants will struggle to compete.

Moreover, these alliances also decreased the odds of a giant building AI capabilities in-house. This is another common issue that keeps CEOs awake at night: "What if Google enters our market?" That's why the best way to grab your executives' attention is to focus on *loss aversion*. This allows you to identify the real must-have partners. How can an alliance protect us against competitors and new market entrants?

As we all know, however, the best defense is a good offense. Once you have gone through the *loss aversion* questions, it is time to flip the script: "Which alliance could allow us to leapfrog light-years ahead of the competition?" Here are a few questions to help you come up with a short list of potential alliance partners:

- Where will our future customers be?
- Who are the leaders in those markets?
- Which large companies need you to close product or service gaps?
- Which companies have customer bases that are large and synergetic?
- Who are leaders in new markets you want to enter?

Remember, partnerships are relationships formed between companies to create a competitive advantage. The right alliance can be the ultimate competitive advantage. The key here is the word *right*. The best alliance partner might not be obvious. To avoid *shiny partner syndrome*, always consider niche players in your industry as well.

They might not get the same buzz as an alliance with a trillion-dollar company. But there will be less competition for their attention. They have a better understanding of your market and customers. Often, they will also create more actual value for customers compared to the glitz and glamor of a press release. Customers don't care about news articles. They care about business outcomes.

Another rather selfish reason to enter a strategic alliance is the M&A (merger and acquisition) potential of the partner. Acquisitions are a huge risk for the acquiring company. They expend a lot of capital so jobs and often the fate of their own company are on the line. Yet most acquisitions still fail. Partnerships and especially strategic alliances, due to their cross-functional and hyper-involved nature, can be a great way to de-risk an acquisition. Nevertheless, you can't ignore your customers just because a potential partner has deep pockets. But huge bags of cash may tilt the scale in favor of one partner over the other.[115]

Once you've created a short list of potential partners, the main question to answer is: Why now? Remember the *build, buy, partner matrix* in chapter 1. The two factors that drive any company decision are 1) whether a capability is core to their business, and 2) whether it is urgent to add the capability to their offering. In order for a company to partner on a capability instead of building it in-house, your offering can't be core to the partners' business. Yet it still has to be urgent. And to set a giant company in motion, there has to be a lot of urgency.

In 2006, Dan Rose joined Facebook as VP of partnerships. Within six weeks he closed a giant $100 million+ deal with Microsoft. How did he sign the biggest deal in his career so fast?

At the time, MySpace had 10x more users than Facebook. It had also signed a $1 billion advertising deal with Google. However, through his connections, Dan knew that Microsoft had been left at the altar when MySpace signed the deal with Google. He saw an opportunity to be their rebound date.

Facebook was the #2 in the social media advertising market. There weren't many deals left that could have offered this type of scale. Dan told Microsoft to move fast. Google was interested in the deal as well. What he didn't mention, however, was that Facebook was wary of Google's own social media efforts, Google+. They strongly preferred Microsoft. So they aligned themselves with Microsoft's ad platform, ambition, a key strategic initiative at the time, and greased the corporate wheel with FOMO (fear of missing out).

Microsoft signed the deal in record time. The partnership was such a success that Microsoft even led Facebook's $15 billion Series C investment round.[116] A huge win for Microsoft given Facebook's market cap of over $1 trillion in 2024.[117]

As a startup it is next to impossible to create the urgency needed to move a giant. It has to come from the outside. So to understand what pressures create urgency for your potential alliance partners, you need to understand the context they operate in. Earlier in this book, we discussed using a *SWOT analysis* to understand the strengths and weaknesses (core activities) as well as opportunities and threats (urgency) of your own company. Alliances can seal the fate of your startup, so you have to get the foundations right. Try to recreate a *SWOT analysis* and *build, buy, partner strategy* for potential alliance partners.

This is easier said than done. Giants like Microsoft have hundreds of business units, each with their own goals and internal politics. It's close to impossible to figure out what they care about from the outside. So your main objective at this stage is to get a hunting license from your own executives. There needs to be enough interest to support your alliance efforts for two to three quarters.[118] Then the real work begins: your fact-finding mission. You have to find the right teams and initiatives to align with.

WHERE TO FIND THE PIECES OF
THE ALLIANCE PUZZLE

When I first read about the Facebook and Microsoft alliance, I immediately wondered: How did Dan Rose know Microsoft was desperate for a deal? How did he get the ear of Microsoft CEO Steve Ballmer so fast and close a deal in six weeks?

Dan shared this story in great detail on Twitter/X where he left a hint: "[Microsoft] bid more than Google for the right to run banner ads, but MySpace was owned by NewsCorp and Rupert liked Google better. Ballmer was reportedly very upset about losing, so my first call was to some folks I knew at Microsoft."[119]

Dan was a known entity. He had spent the past seven years as Jeff Bezos' director of business development at Amazon. He had existing contacts across the ads industry and deep knowledge about the priorities of each major player. Does this mean you need existing contacts at your potential alliances partner to strike a deal?

In 2023, Microsoft had 221,000 employees and hundreds of business units.[120] At this scale, the right arm doesn't know what the left hand does. Even employees of these giants often struggle to articulate what their own priorities are and how they fit into the big picture.

Occasionally, your partner will have clear company-wide priorities. Like in the PandaDoc and HubSpot alliance we discussed in chapter 4. HubSpot's number one priority was to show that free customers would upgrade to paid plans. This was the metric PandaDoc would influence.

Yet in most cases, it's a fool's errand to try to align with the overall objective of your potential alliance partner. If you ask them what their main metric is, they'll likely say: "We want the stock price to go up." But how can a startup expect to influence a trillion-dollar market cap?

Instead, the secret to strategic alliances is to find specific people and teams within the giant who you can align yourself with. Even better if this team is considered crucial by the CEO. In the case of Dan Rose, he built a network of advertising professionals during his time at Amazon. He knew the right people he could contact once an opportunity arose. Actually, he knew the right people who could even let him know there was an opportunity at all!

Strategic alliances are the champions league of partnerships. It is one thing to identify the right opportunity. It is another to have access to the right people to make it happen. This is why the people in charge of these deals tend to be seasoned veterans with a black book of contacts they can reach out to.[121] But don't worry. If you don't have this rolodex of contacts, there still is a way. The hard way.

In late 2018, the customer experience automation tool ActiveCampaign wanted to move upmarket. Tackle larger customers. Who better to form an alliance with than CRM giant Salesforce? With over 150,000 customers and several skyscrapers across the globe, Salesforce was the big fish. The only problem? While ActiveCampaign had some shared customers with Salesforce, their main focus was small businesses. Worse, Salesforce had its own marketing automation platform, Pardot. On the surface, there was no opportunity to partner.[122]

Shay Howe, at the time the VP of design at ActiveCampaign, decided to take a closer look. He reached out to his network and company executives to ask for introductions to employees at Salesforce. At this stage of the process, any conversation is a win. You are on a fact-finding mission.

If you still have no idea where to start, Bernie Brenner suggests browsing press releases and online articles. Look for information about the company, its partners, and other deals they have done. Any people mentioned could be potential leads. Yet when you reach out to them, never go in for the sale. You just want a deeper discussion about their plans. Gather pieces of information. Form a picture of the inner workings of the giant. Identify which team could champion your cause. Understand how they measure success. Compliment their office décor. That's it.[123]

At the end of every conversation, Shay would ask the same question: "Who else at Salesforce should I talk to?" This led to a chain of introductions. Mark Sochan recommends that you should aim for introductions to product managers. By definition, these people are responsible for the "whole product," with a good understanding of both the business and technical issues they face.[124] Yet at this stage, any conversation can lead to valuable insights that can inform your pitch and approach.

At some point, this process will feel like banging your head against a wall. But even at the most impenetrable company, there will always be an entrepreneurial employee who loves to talk to startups. They do exist. If nothing works, try former employees or people who partner with your target company already. Lips are looser when a salary isn't at stake.

When you find friendly faces, follow up regularly. As mentioned before, you never know when the right time for an alliance arises. The only way to measure success at this stage is through progress. What are you learning? Who are you connected with who could inform you if an opportunity arises? Stay top of mind with them. With strategic alliances, you have to gather lots of small wins that result in one large win eventually. It's not a linear engagement, but an exponential one. Persistence pays.

After several months, Shay was introduced to Xiaofei Zhang who worked on a new product: Salesforce Essentials. Behind the scenes, Salesforce built a "light" version of its CRM for small businesses to stave off competition from HubSpot. Their issue? Small customers needed marketing automation, but there was no plan for "Pardot light." Salesforce had to partner. Bingo![125]

By the time they met, Shay had had countless conversations. He spoke Salesforce's language. "Can you share your V2MOM?" This is Salesforce's internal planning framework. He knew when Salesforce's planning cycles started, so he could conveniently be in town a month before to meet up with the team. The pieces started to fall into place.

Shay had also spent months going through the standard onboarding process to the Salesforce app exchange. That's right. You still need to follow the official routes to show you abide by the giant's rules. But an alliance is like a startup within a startup. You are the entrepreneur. Don't let bureaucracy and gatekeepers hold you back. Work the official and unofficial routes in parallel. Collect tiny bits of information to piece together your pitch.[126]

The pitch for a strategic alliance is different from a sales pitch. Your goal is not to share a detailed solution. It's to sell the partner on a vision of the future. What shift is happening in the market and how will we win together in this new world? What leadership coach Andy Raskin calls your *strategic narrative*.[127]

As discussed, you as a startup are too small to move a giant. The big shift has to come from the outside, the market the giant operates in. Your *strategic narrative* has to be centered around a big, undeniable shift in the market. It then paints a vision of how your two companies can thrive together in this new environment. Most importantly, it answers the questions: "Why now?"

For Salesforce, the undeniable shift was an increase in competition from the lower end of the market. Traditionally, small businesses would use cheaper, less customizable CRM products at first. Once they outgrew these products, they upgraded to Salesforce. Yet as these competitors matured, they wanted to hold onto these growing customers. So they launched enterprise offerings. Salesforce Essentials was an attempt to get customers into the Salesforce ecosystem earlier. The same ecosystem ActiveCampaign tried to become a part of.

ActiveCampaign's pitch got the Essentials team interested. The momentum started to build, but they still didn't leap onto the opportunity to partner. Shay had to uncover the rules the Essentials team had to play by. The goals and metrics they were measured on. He had to get the team talking.

In his book *Fishing for Whales,* Sam Hemphill shares 14 techniques to sell into giant companies. One of his fundamental lessons: "People don't pay attention to boring things."[128] To get people talking, make sure that meeting you is the highlight of this person's day. Employees of large companies often feel like cogs in a machine. Work is boring. So they want to spend time with fun and exciting people. Even better if they also have something that might make them look good at work, too!

Early at Hopin, I sold a $120,000 deal to a giant enterprise customer. I asked them what made them choose us over the competition: "We felt like your team was a better *culture fit.*" Translation: they enjoyed spending time with us more than the competition. It took a year to close this deal and endless hours of meetings. Of course, they wouldn't have wanted to spend so much time with people they disliked.

Shay made up reasons to fly to San Francisco and meet the Essentials team at least once a quarter. Each time, he tried to create a unique and memorable experience for the team and showered them in swag. Word about ActiveCampaign started to spread within Salesforce.

NEGOTIATION, EXECUTION, AND THE HEAVY LIFTING

Swag and fun memories will not get you an alliance, however. You still have to identify your counterpart's objectives and decision makers so you can align with them. Unlike a sales deal, there is no set menu or product that you are offering. Alliances are per definition one-of-a-kind arrangements which are unique to both companies. Even throughout the pitch and negotiation, you will still need to continue your discovery process. Tease out every piece of information that could be useful.

To do this, Shay at ActiveCampaign used a technique which I call the *Eff(ort) Bomb*. One of the ways cults recruit new members is through a technique called *Love Bombing*.[129] New members are showered with attention. They feel like the center of the universe. The cult puts insane amounts of effort into making them feel special. All the attention overwhelms the new member, so they want to reciprocate. Once they start to invest, they are hooked.

Of course, your startup isn't a cult. Even though you might all run around in matching swag. But when you drop an *Eff(ort) Bomb* on a partner, the idea is the same. As you might recall from our chapter on marketing partnerships, Shay poured an unreasonable amount of effort into his slide deck. It showcased high-fidelity mockups of 50+ different co-marketing activities for Salesforce and ActiveCampaign. Each with a detailed explanation about its estimated reach.

Some of the ideas were outrageous. The Essentials team said No to almost all of them. But they felt bad about it. Shay had put so much effort into this presentation. So they started to talk. As Shay put it: "Every 'No' leads to 'No' because XYZ." Every explanation was a page of the playbook the Salesforce team had to abide by. Every No got him the information needed to get to Yes.

The activities they did land on exceeded all expectations. Within a few months, ActiveCampaign was the #1 marketing automation partner on the Salesforce app exchange. Ahead of Salesforce's own marketing automation product, Pardot.[130]

In Shay's case, it was his persistence that allowed him to gather a lot of small insights. Pieced together, he was able to create a story that built enough excitement among the Essentials team to form an alliance. Often, however, instead of many tiny insights, you might uncover a *black swan*. This negotiation concept was popularized by former FBI negotiator Chris Voss in his book *Never Split the Difference*. The term *black swan* refers to a rare piece of information that comes as a surprise and has a major impact on your negotiation.[131]

An example of a *black swan* in an alliance negotiation is the story of PandaDoc and HubSpot we discussed in the product partnerships chapter. HubSpot's top priority metric at the time was to convert free customers to paid plans. After a long discovery process, both teams realized that HubSpot customers who closed a single deal were 700% more likely to update to a paid plan! PandaDoc's e-signature solution helped customers sign deals faster. This *black swan* insight was the foundation for a multiyear alliance.[132]

One of the most common mistakes I've seen during alliance negotiations is a lack of focus and preparation. These deals are often negotiated on the CEO level, yet CEOs are busy people. They have a million things going on and never took the time to consider what they really want. This is the moment where all your hard work pays off.

Understand the gives and gets in the negotiation. What are the must-have items? What can we compromise on? What are our alternatives? Most importantly, don't only prepare yourself for the negotiation. You also prepare the other side. Show them what they want. Give them options. Let them choose from the cards you deal.

Preparation always pays off. It requires no talent or intelligence to show up prepared. You just have to do the work. Yet because of the power imbalance between you and the giant the cards might still be stacked against you. In *Dancing with Elephants,* Mark Sochan shares that "large companies often set the rules because they have the power to do so." You have to understand these boundaries and test them or else the elephant will trample all over you.[133]

One of the most common items requested by larger companies is exclusivity. As a startup, this could be a death sentence. If you can only sell to or through one partner, your growth is capped. Worse, the giant can crush you at a whim. It is the ultimate form of *partner concentration risk*.

One of the best examples of the growth an alliance without exclusivity can unlock are Microsoft and IBM. In 1980, IBM was the giant in personal and business computing. It hired the then tiny startup Microsoft to build an operating system called MS-DOS for the IBM Personal Computer. For unknown reasons, IBM did not insist on exclusivity. It had all the power to dictate terms. Yet IBM fumbled the bag.

IBM's distribution made MS-DOS the market standard. Within a year, Microsoft licensed MS-DOS to over 70 other companies. This alliance went down as one the greatest blunders in IBM history. Microsoft, on the other hand, would have never become a multi trillion-dollar company if it had been tied down in exclusivity. It might have withered away together with IBM.[134]

If you can't eliminate exclusivity, try to shorten the term as much as possible. Even six months can be a long time in startup land, but the deal might be worth it. Another awkward topic that will arise in many alliances is indemnification. Who pays when things go wrong? At this stage, the size difference might feel overwhelming.

At Hopin, we sold virtual events software. Clients often poured millions of dollars into the production of their events, but we only saw a small fraction of this money. Still, if our platform went down and the client's event tanked, all their money was gone. So some clients asked us to be liable for damages of $50 million or more. These deals didn't make economic sense.

Yet in alliances, some giants might even ask for unlimited liability. They try to shift all the risk onto the startup. If you take the risk and cause Google's website to go down for even a minute, your startup would be sued out of existence. Alliance partners often ask for these draconian terms because what you think of as a game-changer is only one of many transactions for them. Business as usual.[135]

This can be especially frustrating, since indemnification often only comes up at the eleventh hour. In those moments, the best you can do is try to convince the giant to reconsider. Your top priority as a startup is to stay alive. Even at this stage you have to be willing to walk away.

Another potential headache to get ahead of is customer support. Giants often ask your startup to provide direct customer support (Tier 1) for all issues. Avoid this if you can. The mass of the giant's customer base could crush you. Instead, offer to train their customer support team. Shift the responsibility to supporting their customer support team (Tier 2) and developer support (Tier 3).

It is also important at this stage to have a *joint success plan*, which we discussed in chapter 4. As mentioned earlier in this chapter, startups are often too ambitious at the outset. They immediately aim for the big win. Instead, you should try to break down the alliance into smaller milestones. You don't have to document them in the agreement, but each milestone should de-risk the alliance and unlock more investment from the larger partner.

Remember, you are the entrepreneur. You have to convince the giant to partner with you. Even when the deal is signed and there are high-fives all around, you have to keep their attention. Your work is never done. You have to execute on the deal.

An alliance is a cross-functional effort. A mix of all the previous partnership types discussed in this book. To execute on an alliance means to execute on marketing, service, sales, and product partnerships with the same partner. Revisit the previous chapters for tips on how to execute the different partnerships that compose an alliance. Yet no matter what you do, don't rely on the giant's team for the execution. It is you and your team who have to execute the alliance and prove your worth.

"One big mistake is that a lot of people spend too much time with the partnership team." says Tai Rattigan, COO at Partnership Leaders. You already signed the deal! Get out of the house! Go meet people at the partner organization! Introduce them to counterparts on your team! Meet your partner's partners! Tell them about the alliance! [136]

This process is called *multi-threading* the alliance. The more links there are between your two organizations, the stronger the bond. The last thing you want is that your counterpart quits, and you have to start at square one. Keep up the momentum. As Mark Sochan framed it, your goal is always to "swing to the next partnership vine."[137]

Even the execution phase of the alliance is part of your pitch. Your goal is to gather more data points. These will help you justify additional investment from the alliance partner. It also makes life easier when you pitch an alliance to the next giant.

Eric Chan, former head of partnerships at Chargebee, has an easy way to multi-thread any partnership: invite new team members to each meeting or quarterly business review with the partner. Partnerships are exciting. Team members will always be curious about what is happening behind closed doors. Let them in. Take a peek behind the scenes. Especially if they are relevant to the partnership, but any customer-facing employee will do. This is the easiest way to activate new internal and external champions for your alliance.[138]

For executives, Jared Fuller recommends a different technique: the *circle back play*. For key decision makers like executives on alliance deals, he sends an informal email once a month:

> *"Hey, just FYI, here's what happened here, here, and here. We closed these giant upsells. These things happened. No need to respond. Just letting you know."*

Executives are busy. They have no time to respond. But check the email read receipts. Each email is a touch point to show you are diligent, hardworking, and making progress. In venture capital, there is a saying: "People invest in lines, not dots." One meeting is one data point. A dot. Jared sent eight update emails to Adobe's VP of partnerships before he finally got a meeting which led to a $6 million deal with his company, Drift.[139]

Consistency builds trust and *social capital*. People like to connect the dots and see in which direction the line is trending. Based on these past interactions they can estimate how you will behave in the future. The *circle back play* allows you to create more dots.

This technique also acknowledges two truths about alliances: They take time and involve dozens of stakeholders. Map out the org chart related to the team you partner with. Understand the partner's planning cycles and processes. Then work your way up to meetings with these executives and keep them informed. Every alliance is a mammoth task. It takes a village to move a market.

HOW TO GET YOUR STARTUP ACQUIRED

The goal of an alliance is to become the #1 partner for your category in the partner's ecosystem. If you are the #1 partner, at some point the giant might think "Huh, our customers really like these guys. Maybe we should build something like that, too?"

Even though alliances are multiyear efforts that shift entire markets, eventually almost every alliance comes to an end. This fate is inevitable. Alliance opportunities pop up when an urgent development creates an asymmetry in the market. This is part of your *strategic narrative*. Everything is different! Right now is the time to partner! But the market always seeks balance.

Give it enough time and your competitive advantage from the alliance will erode. Either competitors break into your space, or the giants themselves decide that your capabilities are too important to leave to a partner.[140]

This dynamic explains why Microsoft announced its own in-house Microsoft AI team one year after their big OpenAI partnership. AI is still urgent for Microsoft, but they also want to work on it in parallel in-house. They are the giant. They set the rules.

There is, however, a third option: the giant buys your company and brings your capabilities in-house. But think of the *build, buy, partner matrix* which we showed before as Fig. 3. A partner will move from the *partner* section to the *buy* quadrant when the giant decides that a capability is still urgent but now also is core to their business.

This shift often happens unbeknownst to you. It can be fatal. But since you understand the *build, buy, partner matrix*, you know how to counteract this threat. If a capability is seen as core to the giant's business, their bias will be to build these capabilities in-house. Instead, you have to create urgency and push yourself from the *build* into the *buy* quadrant.

The best way to create urgency in any negotiation is to introduce competition. You should always aim to have more than one potential acquirer. As we discussed, nothing gets a

CEO more rallied up than *loss aversion*. If their competitors want you, the giant will want you too.

However, this is a tactical way to create urgency. The strategic way is to map out how long it would take a company to build your capabilities in-house. Sometimes, it would take too long or even be impossible for them to build these capabilities all by themselves.

At Hopin, we bought seven companies and found that there are three factors that matter during acquisitions: team, product, and market.

Team: How long would it take the acquirer to hire or train a team like yours?

In 2021, Hopin acquired a four-engineer video AI startup called Vectorly. Sam, the founder, and his team had extensive experience in using AI for video enhancements. Instead of hiring our own team to develop these capabilities, we bought an existing team, gave them Hopin sweaters, and called them our in-house video AI team. Sam shared more details about this acquisition in his blog.[141]

These acquisitions are also known as *acqui-hires*. They tend to be on the smaller side. After all, you aren't buying any assets. All you really do is hire the team all at once instead of individually. To sweeten the deal and make sure they also want to be hired, you give them money. Usually in the form of shares in your company. There are people who built their entire career on leaving Google, building a startup, and then being acqui-hired back into Google at a somewhat higher level.

When giants evaluate an acqui-hire, they analyze how difficult it would be for them to hire people with the same experience and skills as your team. Roles that are usually difficult to hire for are executives and engineers. This is bad news for everybody who isn't an engineer.

A large number of non-engineering team members can depress the value of your startup. If you need a lot of sales and service people to deliver value to customers, your margins probably aren't very good. People are expensive. This creates a lot of overhead costs.

If you ever want to go public through an initial public offering (IPO), this will be a problem. Public market investors want to see that most of your revenue comes from scalable software, not people. Any acquirer might also already have a sales team. All they will think of are the severance packages they have to pay to your employees when they lay them off.

Service and channel partners can help. These partners allow you to outsource a lot of the heavy lifting and legwork. This way you can keep your startup lean, nimble, and focused. While it might not be your goal, if push comes to shove, a lean team will always have the option of an acqui-hire as their exit route.

Product: How long would it take the acquirer to build your technology in-house?

As a rule of thumb, a giant company with unlimited resources should be able to build anything in-house. Period. Unless you have some proprietary technology or patents.

Even then, the giant and their army of lawyers will find a way around those obstacles. So why shouldn't the giant launch a copycat of your product?

The most important factor in these situations is urgency. Is it faster and less risky to acquire an existing product vs. build one from scratch? The challenge here is that acquirers often underestimate the time it will take to integrate the new product into theirs.

In 2021, the COVID pandemic had reached its peak. After a year and a half of insane growth in the virtual events market, in-person events were poised to come back. Hopin's customers wanted to know what our hybrid and in-person events offering was. They wanted name badge printing, self-service check-in kiosks, and on-site attendee tracking. An entirely different offering to our virtual events platform.

The market was changing fast, so Hopin decided to acquire one of the top startups in this space, Boomset. While we had dipped our toe in the water with an integration, there were few in-person events we could test our shared offering with. Time was of the essence. We rushed into a deal. This was a mistake.[142]

The two platforms were built in different ways. It was impossible to merge them. Instead, Boomset's capabilities had to be rebuilt from scratch within our platform. Worse, customers rejected the idea of hybrid events altogether. Most wanted to host either an in-person event with Boomset or a virtual event on Hopin. The merger of the two products led to *feature bloat* which made the user experience worse for everybody.

This is a common story, which is why product-centric acquisitions tend to be smaller as well. Product partnerships can help you de-risk these types of acquisitions.

As the acquirer, they allow you to integrate with the potential target company first. You can then get a sense of whether there really is an appetite for your joint solution among your customers. In Hopin's case, customers said they wanted an all-in-one platform for hybrid events. But once they realized that this meant they had to plan two separate events, one virtual and one in-person, few decided to make the investment.

Startups also benefit from integrating first. Even if the acquisition itself fails, the shared customers you win through the product partnership will be a boon for your startup. Because of the tight workflows and integrations between your tools, these customers are also more likely to stick around.

If the initial partnership is a success, it will also attract a lot of attention. The acquirers' competitors are going to pay close attention and smell an opportunity. Their interest will drive up the value of your startup. A larger exit for your team. Nice!

Another way product partnerships allow startups to make them more attractive for an acquisition is simplicity. If you build an all-in-one platform, it is unlikely a giant will want to buy your product. They often want a point solution.

Something that solves one specific issue for their customers and can squeeze right into their own product. More features create more confusion among the acquirer. And a larger risk that the acquisition will fail.

Market: How long would it take the acquirer to capture your customer base and market share?

These tend to be the largest types of acquisitions. They are the least risky. If you are the market leader in your space, I bet you also have a great product and a great team. A giant may launch a copycat but it doesn't mean customers will want it. They still need to find product-market-fit. And large companies are notoriously bad at it.

One of the key features of Hopin's platform was the stage. An interactive webinar-esque experience for large scale presentations. Customers had to use a live streaming tool to host a presentation on the stage. We had built one internally, but live streaming is hard. By definition, everything is live. One mistake and the entire stream drops. At an event, with thousands of people in the audience, the stakes are sky-high.

We partnered with a number of live streaming tools, but the one we always recommended was the market leader, StreamYard. Together with a small team of 19 people, StreamYard's exceptional founders, Dan and Geige, had built one of the most stable and intuitive products on the market. Within one minute anybody could use the tool to create a professional and branded live stream. Something that otherwise would take an entire production crew.

Customers had also voted with their wallets. Two years after launch, StreamYard had scaled to $30 million in annual recurring revenue (ARR) and millions of users. Without any external capital! This explains why Hopin paid a whopping $250 million for StreamYard in January 2021.[143] Despite the high price tag, StreamYard was the most successful acquisition Hopin ever made. It was also the least risky one. The market had already validated StreamYard. All Hopin had to do was let it run as a separate entity in-house.

StreamYard shows us that the most valuable acquisitions happen when a startup exhibits all three types of capabilities that matter to an acquirer: a lean, smart team, a phenomenal product, and a huge customer base the acquirer can cross-sell its product into.

CHAPTER 6:
CRUNCH TIME

"If I have seen further,
it is by standing on the shoulders of giants."
—Sir Isaac Newton

Let's revisit the quote that started the first chapter of this book. Here is what a startup founder posted in a forum:

> *"PARTNERSHIPS could be huge for us if we could figure out what that might look like. Have any of you done any GREAT partnerships that took your business to the next level?"*

Startup founders and employees intuitively get that partnerships can transform their entire business. They see others gain a competitive advantage through partners. But most founders don't understand the fundamental principles that drive these partnerships. Their partner pitch is empty and fake. Like the pacific islanders who started a *cargo cult* to attract airplanes during World War II. These founders wear leaf headphones.

Yet this simple question is the entrance to the rabbit hole that is partnerships. There is so much more to the topic than meets the eye. Because companies don't partner with each other. People do. And people are much more complex than any company could be.

My hope is that next time somebody asks a similar question about partnerships, you are prepared. You know what questions to ask to figure out which department their partners should support. You then grab a napkin and draw out the *build, buy, partner matrix* to help them understand whether partnerships are the right move. Or the *partner value triangle* to determine the value proposition for the customer, the partner, and their company. Or any of the other graphics in this book.

You will look like a genius. Like President Franklin Delano Roosevelt when he jotted down the allied war strategy in World War II on a napkin. Or a mad person. Depending on your drawing skills.

More importantly though, I hope this book showed you how to prevent some of the mistakes I made early in my partnerships career. When our first attempt at a partner program failed because of a bad actor, many CEOs would have pulled the plug. I don't take it for granted that I got a second chance. It led me to do better. To learn from the success stories of the world's best partnership leaders. To understand the principles that drive every partnership.

This experience has allowed me to access an incredibly rewarding career path. When you work in partnerships, your network will explode. Your work is cross-functional. You get to work with different teams at your own company. And all your partner companies. You get to zoom out and view your work as part of the overall company strategy. Given the leverage partners create, it is also common for you to drive millions of dollars in revenue with only a handful of people.

However, the best part of working in partnerships is that we are still early. There are no partner tech unicorn companies. Yet. Large companies have only started to add Chief Partner Officers into their executive teams. For most startups, partnerships are still an afterthought. Often talked about, but too vague to act on.

All this will change soon. Artificial intelligence has already started to flood the internet with synthetic content. AI-generated blogs. Videos. Reviews. Emails. Even video calls. The old way of doing business is dead. When we can't trust any recommendation online, we have to rely on the one source of information we can always trust: partners.

That's why the end of this book should only be the start of your partnership journey. Now is the time to join and help shape the field. I have mentioned resources throughout this book and in the endnotes. If you want to dig deeper into any topic, those are great places to start. I also listed all the partnership leaders mentioned in this book in the acknowledgment. Many of them, including myself, post regular content on LinkedIn. Follow them there and join the conversation.

As promised, there is no sales pitch at the end of this book. No expensive software or course you can buy. The goal of this book was not to make a quick buck. I wrote it because I wish I had a resource like it when I started out in partnerships. But if you enjoyed this book, help spread the word!

Leave a review on Amazon with your favorite insight. Share your copy with a friend. Or casually leave it on the desk of your CEO. They will get the hint. Whatever you do, pay it forward. That is the best part about working in partnerships. You are always on the lookout for ways to grow the pie. Everybody wants to help. Because when you win, we all win. A rising ecosystem lifts all partners.

ACKNOWLEDGEMENTS

As I mentioned in the introduction of this book, I did not write these pages. I curated them. This is the result of hundreds of partnership leaders who took the time to share their insights with me and the industry. Without these people, you wouldn't be reading these lines. And I would have never succeeded in partnerships.

First and foremost, I want to thank Will Taylor. We entered the field around the same time and had countless discussions along the way. His detailed feedback brought out the best sections of this book and made them actionable.

The inspiration for this book came to me after I read several other works by renowned thought leaders like Jared Fuller, Hans Peter Bech, Bernie Brenner, Bob Moore, Mark Sochan, Scott Pollack, Mark Brigman, and Matt Bray. My hope is that this book serves as a foundation for you to now dive into their more technical books.

One thing that made this book special to me is that it gave me a reason to review several hours of interviews I had conducted for my LinkedIn Live Podcast, The Partner Ship. Conversations with experts like Tai Rattigan, Dan O'Leary, Alyshah Walji, Xiaofei Zhang, Nelson Wang, Christine Li, Cory Synder, Marco De Paulis, Olga Lykova, Nick Valluri, Jay LeBeouf, Eric Chan, Aaron Howerton, Antonio Caridad, and Delya Jansen have challenged and refined my thinking on partnerships. I am grateful that we, in a way, got to write *The Book On Partnerships* together. One interview at a time.

I also want to thank Asher Mathews and Chris Samila for creating the Partnership Leaders community. I do not take it for granted that there is a thriving hub where we can meet and push the boundaries of our industry. I have relied on our community for help with some of my most pressing challenges and have made countless new friendships along the way. In particular, my Bay Area chapter co-hosts Shawn Li and Ben Kornfield.

Beyond the books, podcasts, and community, I also had the opportunity to learn from some of the best in the field through conversations or their content. These include Shay Howe, Joe Rice, Ryan Lunka, Michael Nussbaum, Andrew Edelman, Vikram Ghosh, Martin Scholz, Chris Lavoie, Cristina Cordova, Alex Glenn, Sunir Shah, Jill Rowley, Fredrik Mellander, Chris Saad, Jay McBain, Dan Rose, Justin Zimmerman, Ryan Lieser, Greg Portnoy, and Andy

Raskin. Thank you for sharing your knowledge and insights with anybody who is willing to learn.

Finally, I want to thank the Hopin and StreamYard leadership team. Johnny Boufarhat, Armando Mann, Geige Vandentop, Dan Briggs, Andrew Kim, Andrew Beckmann, Brónagh Crowley, and several other members of the Hopin team took a bet on me and partnerships. It has been a wild roller coaster. I wouldn't trade these experiences for anything in the world.

These people have had an impact on me far beyond my professional life. Many of them have become good friends. And that, too, is the beauty of partnerships.

GLOSSARY

1. **Acqui-hire:** The acquisition of a company for the sole purpose of hiring their team.
2. **Affiliate partners:** Partners that market your company to their audience.
3. **Alliance:** Company-defining strategic partnership that touches every department of your organization. The goal of an alliance is to become the #1 partner in your alliance partner's ecosystem for your specific use case.
4. **Asshole:** A bad actor that pushes for a win/lose outcome.
5. **Barney Partnership:** A partnership where two companies get excited about the potential of their collaboration without consulting the end-customer on the value they could derive from the partnership.
6. **Better-Together-Story:** A narrative and pitch about the value proposition of your joint solutions. The goal is to paint a clear picture on why your shared customers

will get more value out of the products or services of your two companies when using them together.
7. **Black Swan:** A piece of information that completely shifts the dynamic of a negotiation.
8. **Buddyware:** A partnership idea rooted in the close relationship between people instead of business rationale.
9. **Business Development:** The process of identifying and validating new strategic initiatives and markets for your business to expand into. This term has unfortunately been co-opted and is often used interchangeably with sales.
10. **Buzzwords:** Specific terms related to your niche that you occupy in a partner's mind and ecosystem. If mentioned, they will trigger your company as the go-to solution.
11. **Cargo Cult:** A person or group of people who imitate behaviors they see others doing in the hope of achieving similar results without an understanding of the underlying systems.
12. **Champions:** People at the partner company who are enthusiastic and eager to engage with you and hold up the partnership flag within their organization.
13. **Channel partners:** Partners that provide a distribution channel for your company.
14. **Channel conflict:** When the principal and partner compete for the same business, usually due to a lack of clarity and guidelines.

15. **Coalition of support:** A group of stakeholders who champion the partnership across both your and the partner's organization.
16. **Co-Intel:** The exchange of information about current or prospective customers.
17. **Co-Marketing:** Joint marketing activities by two or more companies.
18. **Co-Selling:** Joint sales motion by two or more companies.
19. **Customer Concentration Risk:** When a customer controls more than 0.5% of your revenue.
20. **Customer Life Cycle:** The aggregate of an average of 28 touchpoints a customer has with your product throughout their engagement with your company.
21. **Culture Fit:** A formal way of saying that you prefer to spend time and work with a specific person or company over another.
22. **Default Alive:** A state in which your startup is able to survive on the cash flows it generates even if a partnership or fundraise fails.
23. **Ecosystem:** A tight knit web of interactions and connections between companies and partners that contribute to the workflows of a customer.
24. **Eff(ort) Bomb:** The act of flattering your partner with such determination and unreasonable amounts of effort that they will try to reciprocate and help you implement your vision.

25. **Feature Bloat:** When your product becomes too complex and unusable. Usually this happens because you try to do everything yourself and don't focus on your core activities. Also known as the *everything platform trap*.
26. **Integration Platform as a Service (iPaaS):** A platform that allows you to outsource the integration build process and integrate with a large volume of partner companies faster.
27. **Integration Tango:** The awkward dance in a product partnership where both sides try to determine who should build vs. promote a newly built integration.
28. **Independent Software Vendors (ISV):** Technology companies which are part of a larger ecosystem.
29. **Jobs-To-Be-Done:** A framework for understanding the underlying goals and tasks, called "jobs", a customer is really trying to solve with your product or service.
30. **Joint Success Plan:** A shared document that outlines the partnership's path to success.
31. **Key Man Risk:** Risk inherent to partnerships with only one point of contact.
32. **Lock-In–Effect:** Establishing your product as part of an integrated customer workflow which increases your customer's switching cost and the likelihood of their contract renewal.
33. **Marketing Development Fund (MDF):** A form of partner incentive where referral fees from successful deals are invested in joint marketing activities.

34. **Memorandum of Understanding (MOU):** A document which outlines the key terms, goals, and responsibilities which all parties have agreed to.
35. **Minimum Viable Partnership:** Pilot partnership activities to validate initial assumptions.
36. **Multi-threading:** The act of involving two or more points of contact at a partner company in your partnership to minimize key man risks.
37. **Non-disclosure agreement (NDA):** A largely worthless and un-enforceable document. This is not legal advice.
38. **Original Equipment Manufacturers (OEM):** An embedded technology and marketing partner that is an important part of your overall product. A famous example is the "Intel Inside" sticker which was placed on computers from 500+ manufacturers.
39. **Pareto Principle (aka 80/20 Rule):** A phenomenon which states that 80% of the results are delivered by 20% of the inputs and vice versa.
40. **Partner Experience (PX):** The sum of all interactions a partner has with your company.
41. **Partner-licious:** A deal that tastes good to both sides of the partnership.
42. **Partner Concentration Risk:** Risk that comes with one partner controlling an outsized part of your revenue.
43. **Partner-Market-Fit:** The degree to which a partner is a fit for your program and customer base and vice versa.

44. **Post-Mortem:** A document and/or meeting hosted to review all the reasons why failure occurred and to extract learnings from these incidents to improve in the future.
45. **Pre-Mortem**: A document and/or meeting hosted to discuss all the reasons why failure may occur in the future to minimize the chance of these incidents occurring.
46. **Product-Market-Fit:** When your startup is in a good market with a product that can satisfy this market.
47. **Principal:** The company at the center of a partner program or ecosystem.
48. **Referral Partners:** Partners that make referrals and introductions to your company.
49. **Relationship Debt:** The opposite of social capital which occurs when a relationship is damaged and trust is broken.
50. **Return on investment (ROI):** Value captured as the result of an investment in a project.
51. **Risk formula:** Risk = Cost of Failure * Likelihood of Failure.
52. **SaaS Buying River:** A framework which states that customers tend to base their purchase decisions on the tool stack they already acquired and therefore are immune to recommendations for products that are further up the "purchasing stream".
53. **Sales Performance Incentive Fund (SPIFF):** A short term bonus offered to a sales team to encourage them to engage with a new initiative or partnership.

54. **Service Partners:** Partners that provide auxiliary services around your company.
55. **Serviceable Addressable market (SAM):** Opportunity size of a project or partnership that in fact can be serviced.
56. **Serviceable Obtainable Market (SOM):** Opportunity size of a project or partnership that can in reality be obtained.
57. **Shadow Partner Program:** Informal partnerships your team has already established as part of their day-to-day activities and needs, often without realizing.
58. **Shiny Partner Syndrome:** Prioritizing big name partners and flashy logos over real business outcomes when entering a partnership.
59. **Social Capital:** The potential ability to obtain resources, favors, or information from one's personal connections.
60. **Strategic Narrative:** The story of an undeniable shift in the market which creates urgency for both of your companies and the overall partnership.
61. **Supernode:** A company at the center of an ecosystem.
62. **Systems integrators (SIs):** Another term for service partners who offer to implement your product for customers.
63. **Product Partnership:** The go-to-market wrapper around an integration.
64. **Total Addressable Market (TAM):** Total opportunity size of a project or partnership.

65. **Trust Formula:** Trust = Consistency / Time
66. **Value Added Reseller (VAR):** Reseller which sells auxiliary products or services alongside your product.
67. **Hope Value:** The premium investors and acquirers place on your startup because of its sheer potential, even though you have yet to prove you can deliver on it.

ENDNOTES

Preface

1. Stothard, Michael. 2021. "Hopin is officially Europe's fastest growing startup of all time." Sifted. https://sifted.eu/articles/hopin-fastest-growing-startup.

Introduction

2. Wilhelm, Alex. 2021. "Hopin buys livestreaming startup StreamYard for $250M as it looks to expand its product lineup." TechCrunch. https://techcrunch.com/2021/01/07/hopin-buys-livestreaming-startup-streamyard-for-250m-as-it-looks-to-expand-its-product-lineup/.
3. "LinkedIn invests in Hopin, betting on post-pandemic remote events." 2021. CNBC. https://www.cnbc.com/2021/06/09/linkedin-invests-in-hopin-betting-on-post-pandemic-remote-events.html.
4. Brigman, Mark. 2017. Partnernomics: The Art, Science, and Processes of Developing Successful Strategic Partnerships. N.p.: CreateSpace Independent Publishing Platform
5. "Inspired and powered by partners - The Official Microsoft Blog." 2019. Microsoft Blog. https://blogs.microsoft.com/blog/2019/02/05/inspired-and-powered-by-partners/.

6. Fuller, Jared, and Jill Rowley. 2024. Nearbound and the Rise of the Who Economy. N.p.: Independently published.

Chapter 1: Partnership 101

7. Feynman, Richard P. 1986. "Surely You're Joking, Mr. Feynman!": Adventures of a Curious Character. Edited by Ralph Leighton and Edward Hutchings. N.p.: Unwin Paperbacks.
8. Brigman, Mark. 2017. Partnernomics: The Art, Science, and Processes of Developing Successful Strategic Partnerships. N.p.: CreateSpace Independent Publishing Platform.
9. "Whale Watching: The Amazingly Awkward $13B Alliance between Microsoft and OpenAI." n.d. nearbound.com. Accessed July 26, 2024. https://nearbound.com/resources/whale-watching-the-amazingly-awkward-13b-alliance-between-microsoft-and-openai/.
10. Hu, Krystal. 2023. "ChatGPT sets record for fastest-growing user base - analyst note." Reuters. Accessed July 26, 2024. https://www.reuters.com/technology/chatgpt-sets-record-fastest-growing-user-base-analyst-note-2023-02-01/.
11. Scholz, Martin. Comment on "People Think Everything Is A Partnership" by Franz Josef Schrepf. LinkedIn, January, 2024. Accessed July 26, 2024. https://www.linkedin.com/posts/franz-josef-schrepf_partnerships-partnerprograms-businessdevelopment-activity-7155231122824548353-ZYv4/.
12. Check out www.partnerplaybooks.com for webinars and other resources on all things partnerships.
13. Brigman, Mark. 2017. Partnernomics: The Art, Science, and Processes of Developing Successful Strategic Partnerships. N.p.: CreateSpace Independent Publishing Platform.
14. Ghosh, Vikram. "Definition of strategic alliances." In Partnerships Leaders Panel: Strategic Alliances: Where to begin. Webinar, 2022. YouTube video. Accessed July 26, 2024. https://youtu.be/Q8V4B_a3UE0?si=4sjTdoMsow6NjrFT&t=655.

15. Bernhard Friedrichs created a great graphic which lists out even more types of partnerships here: https://partnerstandard.com/partner-types-and-partner-categories/
16. Snyder, Cory. "CSA Masterclass - How I grew my partner program by 500% in 6 months." Cloud Software Association. 2023. Accessed July 26, 2024. https://www.youtube.com/watch?v=QCSkdnqsQDM
17. Lavoie, Chris. "Guidance: Ensuring the future of partner management." Interview by Barrett King. Outcomes - Where Partnerships & SaaS Meet, Podcast, 2023. Accessed July 26, 2024. https://www.youtube.com/watch?v=q7lzVcXFhNM.
18. Portnoy, Greg. "Track & Hack Your Partner Program To $25M ARR w/ Greg Portnoy, CEO at Euler." Interview by Franz Schrepf. The Partner Ship Podcast, 2024. https://www.linkedin.com/events/7176956284653481984. Accessed July 26, 2024.
19. The biggest mistakes companies make in their first year of their partner program journey, Joe Rice (2023). Accessed July 26, 2024. https://www.linkedin.com/pulse/biggest-mistakes-companies-make-first-year-partner-program-joe-rice
20. Brenner, Bernie. 2014. The Sumo Advantage. N.p.: Momentum@work Press.
21. Lafley, Alan G., and Roger L. Martin. 2013. Playing to Win: How Strategy Really Works. N.p.: Harvard Business Review Press.
22. Fuller, Jared. "Stop Playing Sales In Hard Mode." LinkedIn, 2023. https://www.linkedin.com/posts/jaredfuller_nearbound-outbound-sales-activity-7087444280260050945-0bm9/. Accessed July 26, 2024.
23. Pollack, Scott. 2018. *What, Exactly, Is Business Development? A Primer on Getting Deals Done.* N.p.: Independently Published.
24. Dancing with Elephants: The Art of Strategic Partnerships, Mark Sochan, (2018).
25. Pollack, Scott. "Build vs. Buy vs. Partner." LinkedIn, 2023. https://www.linkedin.com/posts/slpollack_build-vs-buy-vs-partner-ideally-thats-activity-7140721809376579585-klPi/. Accessed July 26, 2024.

26. If you aren't familiar with the SWOT analysis, I highly recommend you watch HBO's Silicon Valley, Season 2, Episode 6. For educational purposes, of course.
27. Field, Dylan, and Evan Wallace. 2022. "Adobe to Acquire Figma." Adobe. https://news.adobe.com/news/news-details/2022/Adobe-to-Acquire-Figma/default.aspx.
28. de Paulis, Marco. "From 0 to $10M with the Partner Pipeline King." Interview by Franz Schrepf. The Partner Ship with Franz Schrepf, 2023. https://www.linkedin.com/events/7040338675028606977. Accessed July 26, 2024.
29. Doerr, John. 2021. *Speed & Scale: An Action Plan for Solving Our Climate Crisis Now*. N.p.: Penguin Random House Audio Publishing Group.
30. *The Mom Test: How to talk to customers & learn if your business is a good idea when everyone is lying to you*, Rob Fitzpatrick (2013). A must-read on customer-development for any startup founder and partnership leader.
31. Wang, Nelson. "One of the key lessons I learned building a partner program from ZERO to $100M." Partner Principles (blog), 2023. https://www.partnerprinciples.com/blog/zeroto100m. Accessed July 26, 2024.
32. Wang, Nelson. "The 3 Key Partner Principles: Lessons from 17 years in partnerships." Interview by Franz Schrepf. The Partner Ship Podcast, 2023. https://www.linkedin.com/events/7139022535987249152/. Accessed July 26, 2024.
33. Rattigan, Tai. "007: Tai Rattigan • VP of Business Development at GGV Capital." The Partnered Podcast, 2020. https://partneredpodcast.com/episodes/007-tai-rattigan-vp-of-business-development-at-ggv-capital. Accessed July 26, 2024.
34. You can find the poll and following debate in this Linkedin post: https://www.linkedin.com/posts/franz-josef-schrepf_partnership-alliances-startups-activity-7074739763647270913-dv-X/
35. Cordova, Cristina. "Partnership Principles for Startups" Medium. 2018. https://medium.com/@cjc/partnership-principles-for-startups-36a863e4deb1. Accessed July 26, 2024.

36. Glenn, Alex. "When is the ideal time for tech startups to invest in partnerships?" Linkedin. 2023. https://www.linkedin.com/pulse/when-ideal-time-tech-startup-invest-partnerships-alex-glenn/. Accessed July 26, 2024.
37. LeBeouf, Jay. "The Three Secrets Startups Need to Know to Win Huge Alliance Deals." Interviewed by Franz Schrepf. The Partner Ship with Franz Schrepf. 2023. https://www.linkedin.com/events/7071854652991897600/. Accessed July 26, 2024.
38. "Pmarchive · The only thing that matters." 2007. Pmarchive. https://pmarchive.com/guide_to_startups_part4.html.
39. Ellis, Sean, and Morgan Brown. 2017. *Hacking Growth: How Today's Fastest-Growing Companies Drive Breakout Success*. N.p.: Crown.
40. Rice, Joe. Comment on Franz-Josef Schrepf's post. LinkedIn, July 24, 2023. https://www.linkedin.com/posts/franz-josef-schrepf_partnership-alliances-startups-activity-7074739763647270913-dv-X/. Accessed July 26, 2024.
41. On this note, there's an excellent blog post on how Rahul Vohra, CEO of Superhuman, found PMF using what he calls a product-market-fit engine: https://review.firstround.com/how-superhuman-built-an-engine-to-find-product-market-fit
42. Fuller, Jared. Comment on Franz-Josef Schrepf's post. LinkedIn. 2023. Accessed July 26, 2024. https://www.linkedin.com/posts/franz-josef-schrepf_partnership-alliances-startups-activity-7074739763647270913-dv-X/.
43. Shah, Sunir. Comment on Franz-Josef Schrepf's post. LinkedIn. 2023. Accessed July 26, 2024. https://www.linkedin.com/posts/franz-josef-schrepf_partnership-alliances-startups-activity-7074739763647270913-dv-X/.
44. Fuller, Jared, and Jill Rowley. 2024. *Nearbound and the Rise of the Who Economy*. N.p.: Independently published.
45. Kenton, Will. "What Is Social Capital?" Investopedia, 2022. https://www.investopedia.com/terms/s/socialcapital.asp.

46. Hoffman, Reid n.d. "How to build trust fast, with Daniel Ek." Masters of Scale. Accessed July 26, 2024. https://mastersofscale.com/daniel-ek-how-to-build-trust-fast/.
47. "LinkedIn invests in Hopin, betting on post-pandemic remote events." 2021. CNBC. https://www.cnbc.com/2021/06/09/linkedin-invests-in-hopin-betting-on-post-pandemic-remote-events.html.
48. Mellander, Fredrik. Comment on Franz-Josef Schrepf's post. LinkedIn. 2023. Accessed July 26, 2024. https://www.linkedin.com/posts/franz-josef-schrepf_partnerships-alliances-partnerprograms-activity-7035238322146836481-ciZL.
49. Gregy Portnoy, CEO at Euler, in fact highlighted 16 different jobs a partnerships leader has to do in this excellent LinkedIn post: https://www.linkedin.com/posts/gregportnoy_the-average-partnerships-leader-has-16-jobs-activity-7154533039102992384-vkgs
50. "What Is the Growth Share Matrix? | BCG." n.d. Boston Consulting Group. Accessed July 26, 2024. https://www.bcg.com/about/overview/our-history/growth-share-matrix.

Chapter 2: Marketing Partnerships

51. Rubin, Rebecca. 2023. "Barbie Marketing Campaign Explained: How Warner Bros Promoted the Film." Variety. https://variety.com/2023/film/box-office/barbie-marketing-campaign-explained-warner-bros-1235677922/.
52. Li, Christine. "How G2 Cracked The Code To Building Alliances with AWS, SAP, and Microsoft w/ Christine Li." The Partner Ship with Franz Schrepf. 2023. YouTube. https://www.youtube.com/watch?v=R08SpUgV3BY.
53. Moorehouse, Isaac. "Customer, Partner, then Activities" approach to co-marketing. LinkedIn. Accessed July 26, 2024. https://www.linkedin.com/posts/isaacmorehouse_which-accounts-which-partners-which-activities-activity-7135285608251297793-M-YX/.
54. Zhang, Xiaofei. "The Inside Story of the ActiveCampaign and Salesforce Strategic Alliance w/ Xiaofei Zhang." The Partner Ship Podcast w/ Franz

Schrepf, 2023. YouTube. https://www.youtube.com/watch?v=OeQjG-eDf0Q&pp=ygUeWGlhb2ZlaSB6aGFuZyB0aGUgcGFydG5lciBzaGlw.

55. Schrepf, Franz. "What Is the SaaS Buying River?" Howdy, Partners! Podcast with Will Taylor, 2023. YouTube. https://www.youtube.com/watch?v=8Cmt-mPffXE.

56. Jansen, Delya. "Why You're Setting The Wrong Partner Goals w/ Delya Jansen." The Partner Ship Podcast w/ Franz Schrepf, 2024. https://www.linkedin.com/events/whyyou-resettingthewrongpartner7217260643127545856/

Chapter 3: Service & Channel Partnerships

57. "New Study Finds Salesforce Economy Will Create 9.3 Million Jobs and $1.6 Trillion in New Business Revenues by 2026." 2021. Salesforce. https://www.salesforce.com/news/press-releases/2021/09/20/idc-salesforce-economy-2021/.

58. Bech, Hans P. 2015. *Building Successful Partner Channels: Channel Development & Management in the Software Industry.* N.p.: TBK Publishing.

59. Guerra Cuhna, Bruno. "Oyster's Odyssey From 0 to $200M Raised And 200+ Thriving Partnerships." The Partner Ship w/ Franz Schrepf, 2023. https://www.linkedin.com/events/7127044674640379904/

60. Rattigan, Tai. "The Art Of Global Expansion Through Partnerships w/ Tai Rattigan @ Deel." The Partner Ship w/ Franz Schrepf, 2023. https://www.linkedin.com/events/7082713534236618752/

61. Bech, Hans P. 2015. *Building Successful Partner Channels: Channel Development & Management in the Software Industry.* N.p.: TBK Publishing.

62. Wang, Nelson. "Partner Swimlanes". Partner Principles, 2023. https://www.partnerprinciples.com/blog/swimlanes. Accessed July 26, 2024.

63. Schrepf, Franz. "7 Lessons I Wish I Had Known Before We Built Hopin's Agency Program." Nearbound.com. 2022. Accessed July 26, 2024. https://nearbound.com/resources/7-lessons-i-wish-i-had-known-before-we-built-hopins-agency-program. Accessed July 26, 2024.

64. Wang, Nelson. "One of the key lessons I learned building a partner program from ZERO to $100M." Partner Principles, 2023. https://www.partnerprinciples.com/blog/zeroto100m Accessed July 26, 2024.
65. Howerton, Aaron. "Should Santa Bring You A PRM for Christmas?" The Partner Ship Podcast w/ Franz Schrepf, 2023. https://www.linkedin.com/posts/franz-josef-schrepf_prm-partnerops-partnerships-activity-7158836465135685632-Zfvi.
66. Caridad, Antonio. "Should Santa Bring You A PRM for Christmas?" The Partner Ship Podcast w/ Franz Schrepf, 2023. https://www.linkedin.com/events/7141455665763352577/
67. Matt Bray shared this insight during his six weeks "Mastering Strategic Partnerships" masterclass (2023).
68. Bech, Hans P. 2015. *Building Successful Partner Channels: Channel Development & Management in the Software Industry*. N.p.: TBK Publishing.

Chapter 4: Product Partnerships

69. Zhang, Xiaofei. "The Inside Story of the ActiveCampaign and Salesforce Strategic Alliance w/ Xiaofei Zhang." The Partner Ship Podcast w/ Franz Schrepf, 2023. YouTube. https://www.youtube.com/watch?v=OeQjG-eDf0Q&pp=ygUeWGlhb2ZlaSB6aGFuZyB0aGUgcGFydG5lciBzaGlw.
70. Fuller, Jared. "Webinar: How to win strategic alliance partners with market giants, as a startup." Cloud Software Association, 2023. https://www.youtube.com/watch?v=ZwtxdYLyEZg.
71. Ulwick, Tony. "Jobs-To-Be-Done: A Framework For Customer Needs." 2017. https://jobs-to-be-done.com/jobs-to-be-done-a-framework-for-customer-needs-c883cbf61c90. Accessed July 26, 2024.
72. Fitzpatrick, Rob. 2013. *The Mom Test: How to Talk to Customers and Learn If Your Business is a Good Idea when Everyone is Lying to You*. N.p.: CreateSpace Independent Publishing Platform.
73. Zhang, Xiaofei. "Leveraging Major Player Ecosystems On Their Own Terms." Cloud Software Association, 2023. https://youtu.be/za2PUrM2XFM.

74. Schrepf, Franz. "Whale Watching: Inside the +$100M Facebook and Microsoft Alliance." Nearbound.com, 2023. https://nearbound.com/resources/whale-watching-the-inside-story-of-the-100m-microsoft-and-facebook-alliance/. Accessed July 26, 2024.
75. Grenier, Francois. "Measuring The Real Value of Tech Partnerships." Presentation delivered live at Saas Connect 2022 in San Francisco. 2022.
76. Li, Christine. "How G2 Cracked the Code To Building Alliances With AWS, SAP, And Microsoft w/ Chrstine Li." The Partner Ship Podcast with Franz Schrepf, 2023. https://www.linkedin.com/events/7080199371232829440.
77. Lunka, Ryan. "CSA Masterclass - How to Plan Your Integration Strategy for 2021 with Ryan Lunka, Blended Edge." Cloud Software Association, 2021. https://youtu.be/OmzLnt89F-I?si=nRls1mBpSLa3KuNg.
78. Valluri, Nick. "Build or Let Build? Mastering Integrations w/ Nick Valluri @ Dropbox & Coda." The Partner Ship with Franz Schrepf, 2024. https://www.linkedin.com/events/7192238096380301312/.
79. Valluri, Nick. "Build or Let Build? Mastering Integrations w/ Nick Valluri @ Dropbox & Coda." The Partner Ship with Franz Schrepf, 2024. https://www.linkedin.com/events/7192238096380301312/.
80. I always knew this was happening in some form during negotiations. But only when I read about it in Building Successful Partner Channels: In The Software Industry by Hans Peter Beck (2015) did it click for me.
81. You can find a link to a joint success plan template and an in-depth explanation here: https://www.reveal.co/building-a-high-impact-partner-program/how-to-build-a-partner-program-in-7-steps-part-1. Accessed July 26, 2024.
82. Walji, Alyshah. "How To Use PA-BM To Increase Target Account Conversion By 37% w/ Alyshah Walji." The Partner Ship Podcast w/ Franz Schrepf, 2023. https://www.linkedin.com/events/7090157029507391488/
83. Schrepf, Franz. "What is the Saas Buying River? w/ Franz Schrepf." Howdy, Partners! Podcast with Will Taylor. 2023. https://www.youtube.com/watch?v=8Cmt-mPffXE

84. Moore, Bob. 2024. *Ecosystem-Led Growth: A Blueprint for Sales and Marketing Success Using the Power of Partnerships*. N.p.: Wiley.
85. Fuller, Jared, and Jill Rowley. 2024. *Nearbound and the Rise of the Who Economy*. N.p.: Independently published.
86. Lykova, Olga. "5 Ways to Drive Revenue Through Partnerships w/ Olga Lykova @ Monday.com." The Partner Ship Podcast with Franz Schrepf, 2024. https://www.linkedin.com/events/7186794405016567809
87. Snyder, Cory. "How I Grew My Partnerships Program by 500% in 6 Months with Cory Snyder." The Partner Ship Podcast with Franz Schrepf, 2023. https://www.linkedin.com/events/7062403894441594880
88. De Paulis, Marco. "From 0 to $10M with The Partner Pipeline King w/ Marco De Paulis @ Ryder." The Partner Ship Podcast w/ Franz Schrepf, 2023. https://www.linkedin.com/events/7040338675028606977/
89. Walji, Alyshah. "How To Use PA-BM To Increase Target Account Conversion By 37% w/ Alyshah Walji." The Partner Ship Podcast w/ Franz Schrepf, 2023. https://www.linkedin.com/events/7090157029507391488/
90. Cruz, Justin. n.d. "91% of App Revenue Comes from the Top 1% of Publishers, But That Share Is Shrinking." Sensor Tower. Accessed July 26, 2024. https://sensortower.com/blog/top-one-percent-downloads-1h-2022.
91. Saad, Chris. Comment underneath Franz Schrepf's Linkedin Post. 2023. https://www.linkedin.com/posts/franz-josef-schrepf_partnerships-showmethevalue-alliances-activity-6993157217520656384-JAkZ/. Accessed 26 July 2026.
92. Moore, Bob. 2024. *Ecosystem-Led Growth: A Blueprint for Sales and Marketing Success Using the Power of Partnerships*. N.p.: Wiley.
93. Fuller, Jared. "Nearbound Alliances: Surround Industry Giants w/ Jared Fuller." The Partner Ship with Franz Schrepf, 2024. https://www.youtube.com/watch?v=9sgrrtRrWG0.

Chapter 5: Alliances

94. Fuller, Jared. "CSA Masterclass - How to win strategic alliances with market leaders as a startup w/ Jared Fuller." Cloud Software Association. 2022. https://www.youtube.com/watch?v=ZwtxdYLyEZg

95. Schrepf, Franz. "Whale Watching: The Amazingly Awkward $13B Alliance between Microsoft and OpenAI." nearbound.com, 2023. Accessed July 26, 2024. https://nearbound.com/resources/whale-watching-the-amazingly-awkward-13b-alliance-between-microsoft-and-openai.
96. "Google "We Have No Moat, And Neither Does OpenAI."" 2023. SemiAnalysis. https://www.semianalysis.com/p/google-we-have-no-moat-and-neither.
97. Vincent, James. 2016. "Twitter taught Microsoft's AI chatbot to be a racist asshole in less than a day." The Verge. https://www.theverge.com/2016/3/24/11297050/tay-microsoft-chatbot-racist.
98. "End User Marketing and "Intel Inside" - Ingredient Branding." n.d. Intel. Accessed July 26, 2024. https://www.intel.com/content/www/us/en/history/virtual-vault/articles/end-user-marketing-intel-inside.html.
99. Fuller, Jared. "Nearbound Alliances: Surround Industry Giants w/ Jared Fuller." The Partner Ship with Franz Schrepf, 2024. https://www.youtube.com/watch?v=9sgrrtRrWG0.
100. Olson, Emily. 2023. "Google's AI chatbot, Bard, sparks a $100 billion loss in Alphabet shares." NPR. https://www.npr.org/2023/02/09/1155650909/google-chatbot--error-bard-shares.
101. "OpenAI announces leadership transition." 2023. OpenAI. https://openai.com/index/openai-announces-leadership-transition/.
102. Singh, Manish. 2024. "Microsoft hires Inflection founders to run new consumer AI division." TechCrunch. https://techcrunch.com/2024/03/19/microsoft-hires-inflection-founders-to-run-new-consumer-ai-division/.
103. Roth, Emma, and Nick Barclay. 2024. "'Apple Intelligence' is the name of Apple's iOS 18 AI upgrade." The Verge. https://www.theverge.com/2024/6/7/24173528/apple-intelligence-ai-features-openai-chatbot.
104. "Strategic Alliances: Where to Begin." Partnership Leaders, 2022. https://www.youtube.com/watch?v=Q8V4B_a3UE0
105. Bech, Hans P. 2015. Building Successful Partner Channels: Channel Development & Management in the Software Industry. N.p.: TBK Publishing.

106. Sochan, Mark. "CSA Masterclass - How to Partner with Industry Titans with Mark Sochan." Cloud Software Association, 2023. https://www.youtube.com/watch?v=XCE0EeCLCDo
107. Sochan, Mark. 2018. Dancing with Elephants. N.p.: NAK Publishing.
108. Metz, Cade. 2019. "With $1 Billion From Microsoft, an A.I. Lab Wants to Mimic the Brain (Published 2019)." The New York Times. https://www.nytimes.com/2019/07/22/technology/open-ai-microsoft.html.
109. Brigman, Ph.D., Mark. "Strategic Partnerships Mastery: A Deep Dive Into A $5 Billion Mega Alliance w/ Mark Brigman, Ph.D., SPLP." The Partner Ship with Franz Schrepf, 2023. https://www.linkedin.com/events/7120933795599458304
110. Brenner, Bernie. 2014. The Sumo Advantage. N.p.: Momentum@work Press.
111. Shu, Catherine. 2014. "Google Acquires Artificial Intelligence Startup DeepMind For More Than $500M." TechCrunch. https://techcrunch.com/2014/01/26/google-deepmind/.
112. Redmond, Tony. 2022. "Office 365 Number of Users Reaches 345 Million Paid Seats." Office 365 for IT Pros. https://office365itpros.com/2022/04/28/office-365-number-of-users/.
113. Vailshery, Lionel S. 2024. "Office 365 company usage by country 2024." Statista. https://www.statista.com/statistics/983321/worldwide-office-365-user-numbers-by-country/.
114. "Amazon completes $4B Anthropic investment to advance generative AI." 2024. About Amazon. https://www.aboutamazon.com/news/company-news/amazon-anthropic-ai-investment.
115. Sochan, Mark. 2018. Dancing with Elephants. N.p.: NAK Publishing.
116. Schrepf, Franz. "Whale Watching: The Inside Story of the +$100M Microsoft and Facebook Alliance." nearbound.com, 2023. Accessed July 26, 2024. https://nearbound.com/resources/whale-watching-the-inside-story-of-the-100m-microsoft-and-facebook-alliance.
117. "FB: Meta Platforms Inc Stock Price Quote -." n.d. Bloomberg. Accessed July 26, 2024. https://www.bloomberg.com/quote/FB:US.

118. Partnership Leaders. "Strategic Alliances: Where to Begin." Partnership Leaders, 2022. https://www.youtube.com/watch?v=Q8V4B_a3UE0
119. Rose, Dan. X Thread about the full Facebook and Microsoft Alliance Story. Twitter/X, Nov 20, 2020. https://x.com/DanRose999/status/1330215611666980864. Accessed July 26, 2024.
120. "Microsoft." Wikipedia. Accessed July 26, 2024. https://en.wikipedia.org/wiki/Microsoft.
121. Fuller, Jared. "Nearbound Alliances: Surround Industry Giants w/ Jared Fuller." The Partner Ship with Franz Schrepf, 2024. https://www.youtube.com/watch?v=9sgrrtRrWG0.
122. Ramirez, Olivia. 2020. "ActiveCampaign's Co-Marketing Playbook for Getting the #1 Spot in Salesforce's AppExchange." Crossbeam Insider. https://insider.crossbeam.com/resources/activecampaigns-co-marketing-playbook-salesforces-appexchange.
123. Brenner, Bernie. 2014. The Sumo Advantage. N.p.: Momentum@work Press.
124. Sochan, Mark. 2018. Dancing with Elephants. N.p.: NAK Publishing.
125. Zhang, Xiaofei. "The Inside Story of the ActiveCampaign and Salesforce Strategic Alliance w/ Xiaofei Zhang." The Partner Ship Podcast w/ Franz Schrepf, 2023. YouTube. https://www.youtube.com/watch?v=OeQjG-eDf0Q&pp=ygUeWGlhb2ZlaSB6aGFuZyB0aGUgcGFydG5lciBzaGlw.
126. Fuller, Jared. "Nearbound Alliances: Surround Industry Giants w/ Jared Fuller." The Partner Ship with Franz Schrepf, 2024. https://www.youtube.com/watch?v=9sgrrtRrWG0.
127. Raskin, Andy. 2017. "The Making of a Great Strategic Narrative | by Andy Raskin | Mission.org." Medium. https://medium.com/the-mission/the-making-of-a-great-sales-narrative-978938b3926.
128. Hemphill, Sam. 2021. "Fishing for Whales: 14 Prospecting Principles for Enterprise Sales." SkyCenter, LLC.
129. Montell, Amanda. 2021. Cultish: The Language of Fanaticism. N.p.: HarperCollinsPublishers.
130. Zhang, Xiaofei. "The Inside Story of the ActiveCampaign and Salesforce Strategic Alliance w/ Xiaofei Zhang." The Partner Ship Podcast w/ Franz

Schrepf, 2023. YouTube. https://www.youtube.com/watch?v=OeQjG-eDf0Q&pp=ygUeWGlhb2ZlaSB6aGFuZyB0aGUgcGFydG5lciBzaGlw.
131. Voss, Chris, and Tahl Raz. 2016. Never Split the Difference: Negotiating As If Your Life Depended On It. N.p.: HarperCollins.
132. Fuller, Jared, and Jill Rowley. 2024. Nearbound and the Rise of the Who Economy. N.p.: Independently published.
133. Sochan, Mark. 2018. Dancing with Elephants. N.p.: NAK Publishing.
134. Fadell, Tony. 2022. Build: An Unorthodox Guide to Making Things Worth Making. N.p.: HarperCollins Publishers.
135. Sochan, Mark. 2018. Dancing with Elephants. N.p.: NAK Publishing.
136. Rattigan, Tai. "Tai Rattigan, Global Head of Partnerships at Deel and Co-Founder at Partnership Leaders - The Magic Partnering Well." The Michael Girdley Show Episode 46. Spotify, 2022.
137. Sochan, Mark. 2018. Dancing with Elephants. N.p.: NAK Publishing.
138. Chan, Eric. "How CSMs can leverage Partnerships to increase NRR by 40% w/ Eric Chan." The Partner Ship Podcast w/ Franz Schrepf, 2023. https://www.linkedin.com/events/7133915169109262336/.
139. Fuller, Jared. "Nearbound Alliances: Surround Industry Giants w/ Jared Fuller." The Partner Ship with Franz Schrepf, 2024. https://www.youtube.com/watch?v=9sgrrtRrWG0.
140. Sochan, Mark. 2018. Dancing with Elephants. N.p.: NAK Publishing.
141. Bhattacharyya, Sam. "How Vectorly Joined Hopin." Vectorly Blog, 2021. https://medium.com/vectorly/how-vectorly-joined-hopin-93dffdb1acc4. Accessed July 26, 2024.
142. Neves, Miguel. "Hopin Acquires Boomset in Bid to Conquer Hybrid and In-Person Events." Skift, 2021. Accessed July 26, 2024. https://meetings.skift.com/hopin-acquires-boomset-bid-conquer-hybrid-person-events/.
143. Wilhelm, Alex. 2021. "Hopin buys livestreaming startup StreamYard for $250M as it looks to expand its product lineup." TechCrunch. https://techcrunch.com/2021/01/07/hopin-buys-livestreaming-startup-streamyard-for-250m-as-it-looks-to-expand-its-product-lineup/.

ABOUT THE AUTHOR

Franz-Josef Schrepf is best known as the Director of Strategic Partnerships at StreamYard and Hopin, a live streaming and virtual events company which Sifted called "Europe's fastest growing startup of all time." He joined Hopin as employee #16 and contributed to its meteoric rise, including:
- $1B in funds raised at a $7.75B valuation.
- over 1,200 employees hired at its peak.
- 7 acquisitions including the live streaming platform StreamYard at $250M.
- hundreds of channel, service, and technology partnerships established.
- several alliance deals, including an investment of up to $50M from LinkedIn.

He is a frequent contributor and speaker on the topic of partnerships on podcasts, blogs, events, and conferences as well as the host of one of the most popular partnership podcasts, The Partner Ship.

Originally from Germany, Franz-Josef lives with his wife and daughter in San Francisco where he is one of the Bay Area chapter hosts of the Partnerships Leaders community.

Made in the USA
Columbia, SC
22 August 2024